Compassion Haiku

Daily insights and practices for developing
compassion for yourself and for others

By Karl Grass

Text Copyright © 2013 Karl Grass

All Rights Reserved. No part of this book may be
reproduced in any form or by any means,
electronic or mechanical, including photocopying,
recording, or by any information storage and
retrieval system, without permission in writing
from the author.

Dedication

Tapestry of love
Holds all with gentle embrace
Each strand is precious

• • •

This book is dedicated to my family: Kathy, Andrew, Jennifer, and Michael.

Preface

Compassion: *Sympathetic consciousness of others' distress together with a desire to alleviate it*
-     Webster's New Collegiate Dictionary

The inspiration for this book came from a conversation with a good friend, Linda Newlin, who had just described for me the vision that tapped an amazing font of creativity from inside her. She had just finished writing her first CD and was planning a one-woman show. The focus of her work was about loving yourself and saying, "no" to help end abuse. It immediately hit me how important self-compassion is. Without it, abusive relationships continue. With it, more people say, "no" and do what is needed to get out of the horrible situations they find themselves. Imagine how much suffering in the world would end if we all became more self-compassionate.

For some years prior to this I had been working to boost my own level of self-compassion and had been on the lookout for ways to increase it. The conversation with Linda gave me an idea; what if I reflected on it everyday and wrote about what I learned and tried that day? I had journaled quite a bit and knew from experience that regular reflection was helpful. The idea of a daily haiku coupled with some short comments appealed to me. That way I could capture something of both the experiential and intellectual nature of what I had encountered each day. And with no further thought I started that day and continued each day thereafter until a full year had gone by.

Surprisingly, I never hit the dreaded "writer's block." Many nights I sat down with my laptop and had no idea what I would write. Yet, after reflecting on the day, something invariably came up. Sometimes I had a felt sense of the insight and working to reflect it in a haiku helped bring out the rational side. Sometimes it was the logical understanding that was clear and I worked to get in touch with the essence and express a more experiential form of it in a haiku. And, of course, some are more successful than others.

As I continued I found my focus shifting from mostly self-compassion to compassion for others. What I see more clearly now is how tightly bound the two are. As my self-compassion became stronger, my capacity for compassion for others grew. My hope is that you will experience the same.

Although the writing of this was a self-development activity I decided to publish it in the hope that it might benefit others. This wish is true for each reader and for our broader world. I hope it can become a resource for anyone looking to increase his or her own capacity for compassion. If it offers a chance for your own use of reflection and supports your own experiments in compassion it will have met its mark.

More broadly, it is clear to me that compassion is the most effective and practical means we have for ending suffering in our lifetime. It is available to each of us all of the time, no money is required to develop it, no laws or regulations are needed to use it, and no limitations in science or technology are holding us back. Making it a daily practice is all that is required to literally change the world.

The image of a world where abusers care enough for themselves and others that they can no longer tolerate being a source of pain and where those being abused are self-compassionate enough to get themselves out of harm's way when they can is a powerful one. Imagine all of the ills that will end when we each take up the mantle of living compassionately. There is literally no limit and my wish is that this is enough to motivate you to start today.

For anyone reading this who is wondering if all of this isn't just a bit too lofty I'd like to offer a more mundane example. Consider how compassion and capitalism can meet.

The very heart of capitalism is an exchange between parties where each receives something of greater value than what they gave up. Here is where compassion can make such a difference. The more in touch we are with someone else's challenges, the better we will be at helping overcome them. And the better we are at overcoming them, the greater the value we provide. And the greater the value we provide, the more likely we will not only do good but that we will also prosper and build a loyal customer base in the process.

My suggestion for working with this material is that you set aside a short amount of time each morning and approach each day's haiku and commentary with a spirit of contemplation and an intention to make compassion a part of your day. Each day's words should be read slowly. While it is certainly possible to read ahead or to read sections at a time, I am not sure this will be as meaningful as taking in the material gradually, one day at a time.

If you prefer to sample a page at random each day I certainly invite you to do so. However, there are a few sections where I suggest some multi-day practices. If you run across one of these you may

want to stay with the sequence that contains them
until the practice is complete.

• • •

End of the path looms
Sweet nostalgia arises
New travels begin

Acknowledgments

I'd like to thank those who helped encourage me and who directly or indirectly supported this venture. These include all of the many folks at the Hudson Institute of Coaching. Especially Toni McLean, Pam McLean, Sandy Smith, John Schuster, and Kathleen Stinnett who ostensibly introduced me to coaching but who really set me on a path of life long learning and exploration. That has been a tremendous gift. Pat Adson, my coach and heartfelt journey guide, deserves great credit for helping me walk the path of self-development. It is due to that work that I was able to even consider putting this work, which started as private thoughts, out there. Linda Newlin, who I mentioned in the Preface, was a regular source of encouragement as the many months between beginning and end passed by.

Throughout all of the writing my family gave me plenty of space to complete this work despite the fact that it often kept me up late or had me sequestered in my office during the evening. Despite my occasionally staring into my laptop and typing sporadically during family movie nights, they respected my privacy and never distracted me by trying to look over my shoulder or get a sneak peek. In short, they let me get comfortable with what I was writing on my own terms. This was not only welcome but helped me protect my fragile ego while the work was evolving.

I have no doubt my thinking about compassion has also been influenced by the writings of Pema Chodron and Brené Brown, and by various Buddhist practices and studies I have engaged in as a student of Dzogchen Ponlop Rinpoche and as a member of Nalandabodhi. There is no substitute for learning from others who have traveled the territory while making your own journey.

Two other special thanks are due. First, the calligraphy used in this book is the work of Nao at www.japanesecalligrapher.com and it is due to her kind generosity and permission that it is being used. Second, I have been a regular visitor to www.howmanysyllables.com more times than I can recall. The usefulness of this site in the writing of this book is hard to overstate.

December 2012
Karl Grass
Nokomis, Florida

共感

The Author

Karl Grass lives in Florida with his wife and two sons. He currently works as an executive coach with clients domestically and internationally. He is also a member of the Hudson Institute of Coaching leadership team and helps facilitate their LifeLaunch™ program. Previously he has served as a general manager of various software organizations ranging in size from $25 million to more than $250 million. Along the way he has also been a partner in Arthur Andersen and a co-founder of a software start-up.

When not coaching or writing he is an avid long distance sea kayaker and bicyclist. At this point in time he has successfully kayaked the 271-mile Everglades Challenge, completed various kayaking expeditions in and around Lake Superior and the Everglades, and has finished seven 100-mile century rides.

Karl may be contacted at
karl@compassionhaiku.com.

Table of Contents

January

• • •

Just be with ourselves
Such a simple, gentle way
Calls first for a heart

Just being with ourselves is different from what most of us do. Not judging, just accepting who we are. This is gentler and simpler than how most of us experience ourselves. Our hearts are not critical or judgmental. They are open. They are what allow us to be comfortable standing by our own side just as we are. Name any flaws you have and write them down. Now, practice acknowledging these exist while also reassuring yourself you will support yourself regardless. You can tell yourself something like, "I will be with you while you work with these," or any other words of reassurance that you find helpful.

• • •

Not loving, not lost
Hollowness deep inside me
Time to be present

Limbo is a tough place to be. When we are disconnected from all that is around us and within us we are like ghosts with no substance. If we have no presence, we cannot be compassionate. Acknowledge yourself by noticing your strengths and your accomplishments, no matter how small, as you go through your day.

January 3

• • •

We love others well
If we were our own children
Would we be so hard?

See yourself from another perspective. If you were
your own child, how would you, as the mother or
father to you, see yourself? What would you love
and appreciate? Would you be nearly so hard on
yourself if you were your daughter or son?

January 4

• • •

Warm, intimate glow
Inside me peaceful presence
Me and me fit well

See yourself filled with a warm, soft light and feel
how you are right for yourself. Only you can so
perfectly be you. No one else can match your true
self so well, let that inner sense grow and feel it as
a real presence inside you. Make it your friend and
companion. As you become practiced at
supporting yourself your ability to support others
will become stronger.

January 5

• • •

Where am I all day?
Just catching up with me now
Hello my good friend

Our days can be very busy. That same busyness
can take us away from our awareness. As we
notice more about ourselves we are able to see
and accept more of us. Throughout the day, pause
periodically to be aware of what you are
experiencing and just notice it. This is about
becoming familiar with who we are, the things we
may want to change, and the things we like and
appreciate. Notice them both and become
acquainted with them.

• • •

Remorse and resolve
Don't want to cause suffering
For self or others

What are the ways you contribute to the suffering of others, what are the ways you contribute to the suffering of yourself? Pick one thing to give up each day for the next week. It's a good idea to start small. Maybe it's deciding not to tailgate someone when you are in a rush. Maybe you decide not to roll your eyes when someone says something you think is stupid. Now pick some act of compassion you want to add. For example, you may choose to appreciate something about yourself each day. Whatever you decide, write it down somewhere and put a check mark next to it for each day you succeed.

January 7

• • •

Focusing on self
Quick to notice shortcomings
Fine-tune what is true

How has your daily practice from yesterday gone? What are you noticing as you attempt to let go of something that causes some suffering either to yourself or others? What are noticing as you take on something affirming and compassionate? When I thought my first good thought about myself it stuck for about five seconds before all sorts of objections about why it wasn't true arose in my mind. So, I picked something that was slightly different that reflected more of the essence of what was true about me. It stuck, and I learned something about myself that I can honor. What has your experience been? How can you make it more lasting?

Today is day two of the practice.

January 8

• • •

Honoring what's good
Can it be just that simple?
Now, rinse and repeat!

A practice is just that: practice. It's something you continually do and refine. How is your practice from two days ago progressing? No matter what you've done or haven't done there is something to be learned from that experience and how you respond to it. For example, I've noticed how I put off the practice when it comes to mind, or how I am inclined to just do part of it, "saving" the rest for later! That helped me see how deeply I am resisting being good to myself, and to recognize the antidote, being good to myself!   Simply seeing that gave me new appreciation for the exercise. What are you learning from your practice? How can you use it?

Today is day three of the practice.

January 9

• • •

Chore, not joy; duty
Working my practice is work
It always bears fruit

Today is the fourth day of the practice exercise. It may be going exceptionally well for you. It may feel like a chore. It may not be a big deal. Which is true for you? Whatever is true, there is value in repetition and consistency. It's how we learn and adjust. For those days when being good to yourself and others is uninspiring, remember that keeping the practice alive is still building your capacity and is an act of self-compassion in and of itself.

Today is day four of the practice.

January 10

• • •

Breathing in slowly
Like a warm caress inside
Releases burdens

Make your breath a short escape by sensing it
filling your body and bringing comfort, life, and a
reassuring glow inside. Simply create the
awareness of this with a deeper breath anytime
you choose. Use that interlude as a refreshing
break to take on something that might otherwise
be difficult or has been eluding you.

Today is day five of the practice.

January 11

• • •

I will stand by you
Powerful words for yourself
Moves us to meaning

When we love ourselves we create something that can't be taken away. We create a strong presence as we acknowledge to ourselves that we are worth standing with.

Today is day six of the practice.

. . .

Mirror on the wall
Holds our attention tightly
So much that we miss

We can become oblivious to those around us when we get fixated on ourselves. If we get single-minded about getting ahead and are constantly (even subconsciously) checking our position and standing and status we loose sight of all else. How much we miss! Our child's desire for closeness, an old lady hoping traffic will stop so she can cross the street, a friend's call for advice, our spouse's attempts at warmth, and so much more. It's hard to be compassionate when we get self-absorbed. On days like this we may have to forcefully remind ourselves and practice compassion with intention before all opportunities slip away unnoticed.

Today is day seven of the practice.

January 13

• • •

Solid not rigid
All the layers together
Strength can be subtle

Take in the reality of the changes you practiced this
last week. Appreciate that part of you that was
important enough to you to care for and that cared
enough about others to do something to make
their lives just that much more pleasant. As you do
this, feel that inner sense of strength that you are
nourishing.

January 14

• • •

Love can toughen one
We stand up for those we love
Not those we do not

Sometimes we stereotype love and compassion as being for the weak. Yet when we love something deeply we stand-up to protect it from harm. When danger is present even the meekest mother will put herself between it and the children she deeply loves. This is not weakness, this is strength. What kindness to yourself can you show by standing up for yourself a little more?

January 15

• • •

How high is the bar?
Reaching, reaching we try hard
Why does it matter?

We can get trapped in a belief that we can be perfect and our lives should be just so. The first question might be, "What is important about the perfection we are reaching for and why does it matter?" Can we still be worthy of happiness and contentment without it?

January 16

· · ·

Danger threatens close
Water lapping at the edge
Reinforce the walls

Protecting our boundaries must start before the
danger is severe. When people push our limits of
good will or abuse our generosity we can let them
or we can let them know they have gone far
enough. While we might struggle with doing this
gracefully, the alternative is to let others
strengthen a habit that adds pain to the world and
jeopardizes our wellbeing. When we fail to stand
up for ourselves we weaken our ability to serve and
stand up for others. Recognize when the
boundaries that protect you are at risk and act to
maintain them timely.

January 17

• • •

Getting some things done
Less judgment quickens the day
My needs are served well

Sometimes getting things done can put us in a
better frame of mind. When we get things done
we are serving our needs, a clear act of self-
compassion. And, we are less likely to judge
ourselves harshly, another act of self-compassion.
Pick something to do today that you've been
putting off and get started.

• • •

**Simple acceptance
Like waves belong on water
We are as we are**

There is no need to be more than what is. In fact, that is impossible by definition. We can feel good about being part of the natural order of things and simply accept that we are worthy as we are.

January 19

• • •

Thank you for the day
I worked, ate, rested, and thought
All of which served me

Being thankful when we attend to our own needs is a reminder that we are deserving. Does this strike you as selfish? The definition of being selfish is when you lack consideration of others. If this still strikes you as being selfish, consider how well you are able to serve others when you don't attend to your own needs.

What needs of yours did you meet today that you can give thanks for? Thank yourself as you would a kind friend.

January 20

• • •

Stepping into self
We express our true beliefs
Honor who we are

We find it easier to love what we can respect. We defend what we love. Expressing our true beliefs is an acknowledgment of the respect we have for ourselves. What do you hold back from expressing out of fear that others may not like it? What are you willing to share as a way to honor your self?

January 21

• • •

Warm gratitude grows
Helping myself and others
Notice and hold it

Notice each good deed you do for your self and for others (especially the simple ones.)   Appreciate those kind acts long enough for you to recognize the good you hold.

• • •

First rule, "Do no harm"
Ah! Breathing is easier
Space for love to grow

A first step to being more compassionate is to do less harm to yourself and others. What habits do you have that are actually harmful? Letting go of what doesn't serve you or others alleviates suffering and makes way for a better life. What new habit do you want to develop to take its place?

• • •

Waves of joy move me
A kindness received is bliss
Same from me as you

An unexpected kindness when needed can move us with joy, relief, and gratitude. Others can do it for us. We can do this for others. We can do it for ourselves. Consider all of the acts of kindness you showed yourself and others recently. How many ways did you support your own or someone else's well being? Finishing an old "to-do," listening to a friend, cleaning out a drawer… In every day life we find ways to honor our selves and others. As you lay down tonight, search for each act of kindness and let it warm you.

January 24

• • •

Ugh, this isn't it
Dark and in a deeper hole
But I do see it

Some days we do things that we know are the opposite of what we want. We might want to be compassionate and loving but we aren't. But if we see that is the case we can still be glad we are now in a position to make a choice of how to respond.

January 25

• • •

Comfort as I am
Show up as me, no worries
I like who I am

A benefit of liking yourself is that no one can take
that away unless you let them. It's a good reason
to take the time to appreciate the good that you
do, for yourself and for others. We feel better
about who we are and express ourselves more
authentically as a result.

January 26

• • •

**Wind blows far and wide
Our heart's compassion untamed
Let love speak freely**

Let your heart's compassion grow by sending it
forth across the earth as if carried by the wind.
Feel it being set free to bless everyone it reaches.
Do this every time you feel a breeze on your face or
see the branches of a tree or a flag being brought
to life by the wind. Or simply do it anytime you
want to lift up your heart.

January 27

• • •

The pen is mighty
Labels replace what is real
Words are no less strong

How do you think and talk about yourself? When
we hear messages over and over it can be easy to
take them as being reality. Listen to your self-talk
and the ways you describe yourself to others.
Make an effort to record the messages and the
frequency you hear them in a day. Do they match
what is real? What can you replace them with that
better reflects what is true?

January 28

• • •

Huff, puff, chug, chug, chug...
Not an easy thing this work
A labor of love

If it were easy everyone would do it. Of course, sometimes it is easy. It is when it is hard that the phrase "labor of love" rings true. But our prize is so great. It is nothing less than our own selves, our own sense of worthiness, and the full expression of our humanity and compassion. Use that motivation as encouragement to keep working at generating a heart filled with compassion.

January 29

• • •

**Transformed by deep breath
Space opens and light comes through
A softer moment**

A pause is all that it takes to allow hard emotions
to soften and the light of new possibilities to be
seen and acted upon. In that window we can step
back and question if our automatic reaction is
really what we want to experience and then make
new choices. A pause is always available to us.
Sometimes it is as simple as taking a deep breath.
See how many pauses you can put to use in your
day today. Each one offers an opportunity to put
an end to, or avoid, a measure of suffering.

January 30

• • •

Still missing kindness
Behavior like yesterday
Counting my blessings

Sometime I notice how far I have to go but just
don't feel like dwelling on it. Counting my
blessings is more enjoyable and reminds me of my
basic worth. Rather than dwell on what's not
working try naming everything good about your
day.

• • •

Anger puffs us up
Indignation sure feels good
Until it's over

We'll all had this experience. Despite knowing better, there is an indulgent quality to venting our justified indignation. Of course we are right, of course we should be upset, or angry or demanding or... But then there is the subtle price to pay. Maybe we feel slightly guilty for having dumped on someone else and passing the bad feelings on, or the sour mood that results from continually reminding ourselves why our bad behavior was justified, or continuing to complain and carp to others to get some validation for the way we have been feeling. All of which, just loops back to feed itself and continue the sense of ill being. The more we notice these costs, the less likely we are to get trapped in that initial indulgence.

What tips you off to the fact you've landed in that place? Perhaps it is something physical like pursed lips or a rising heart rate or rapid, shallow breathing. Whatever it is, there is great value in finding that early sign and becoming intimately aware of it when it first arises. Then you can use it to alter course and avoid the costs we all pay for losing the connection to our heart of compassion.

February

February 1

• • •

Greet the day with joy
Quiet wonder, warm embrace
Waiting to be love

How we approach the day can set a tone of
compassion for what comes. Like a child we can
hold quiet wonder and expectation for a day filled
with possibilities. By the simple act of holding love
for what comes next we remind ourselves of what
we are capable of. Right now, imagine the day as a
wondrous expression waiting to happen. And do it
again and again for the next two minutes to see
how our expectations and intention shape our
experience.

February 2

• • •

How can I add joy?
Not giving myself away
Being strong instead

There is no contradiction between being strong
and adding joy. In fact we rarely turn to those who
are weak for our inspiration or a lift in spirits.
When we are strong, we are more capable and
more likely to be in good spirits ourselves. Take
the day to notice when you are strong and when
you are weak. What are the ways you can feed
that strength? Being compassionate to yourself
supports being compassionate to others.

February 3

• • •

Empty and hollow
Anger kills the connection
Love lost, elusive

There are times when our compassion is trampled in anger as we hit out at others in a rage. When the storm is over an important connection is lost and the void between us and the other person leaves us blindly wandering, uncertain what to do next to recover what has been lost. In these dark moments the value of developing our compassionate heart is even more clear and convincing. Let the deep, felt sense of that cost be your motivation to grow your capacity for compassion.

• • •

**Seeing just the best
The cup of love overflows
We are made ready**

We can see others or ourselves as lacking and be upset by it. Or we can choose to want the best for others and ourselves and focus on that. Notice the shift that takes place when we do that. When we are compassionate with others and with ourselves we support better ways of being. And, when we see that vision of a better way of being we can act on it. Take several moments each day, for the next week, to activate your compassion for yourself and others by seeing the best qualities and possibilities of all. Notice what the best looks like for you and make the choices that move you in that direction.

February 5

• • •

Everyday life
Opportunities for love
Stronger and stronger

Everyday we face those moments of
disappointment or even anger. Sometimes it is
with us. Other times it is with others. Each
moment gives us the opportunity to see what could
be and to want that for ourselves or to want that
for others, as the case may be. Did you notice that
today? We first have to notice the discrepancy and
choose a better course before we can act.

Today is day two of the practice.

February 6

• • •

Out in the open
We choose and begin anew
Seeing makes it real

As we get more skilled at noticing our judging of
our self or others we are confronted openly with a
choice. We can see it as an opportunity for love
and compassion. Of course, we don't have to but
ignoring that opportunity is harder than when we
don't see it in the first place.

Today is day three of the practice.

February 7

• • •

Friends and family
Talking, listening, laughing
Life well lived in love

Some days just go smoothly and little is required of us to cope – savor those moments whenever they come.

Today is day four of the practice.

February 8

• • •

Open sky calls us
Be who we are, let all see
Strong, steady, and real

What could be more compassionate than to allow ourselves to gracefully express who we are? When we can live without fear of who sees us, as we really are, we gain our freedom: Freedom to act with certainty, freedom to make our lives ours, freedom to create what is possible. Let the love for your self reach deep and be felt.

Today is day five of the practice.

February 9

• • •

Towering mountain
Silent, like wind, touches all
Humbles and inspires

Our dignity, like our acts, speaks for itself. Our
presence shapes the world. Be like a majestic
mountain; rise above the plain to proclaim what
can be. Nurture your values and gifts and let their
beauty be your source of inner strength.   Find one
way to share a part of your true self today that you
might otherwise hide away.

Today is day six of the practice.

• • •

Electricity!
Current connects and lights up
Build a bigger grid

When our hearts open and we receive the emotions of another it can be like a current running through us. Our ability to connect fully with others depends on our ability to be able to acknowledge and work with our own emotions. The more we can be comfortable with our own emotions, all of them, the more we can handle the emotions of others. What emotions do you ignore, what ones do you embrace, what ones do you want to respond to more effectively?

Today is day seven of the practice. What is the insight you most want to remember from the week?

• • •

Spikes, pain, agony
We are longing for escape
Forgiveness frees us

Forgiveness is compassion after the fact. We let go
of the burden we have accepted or put on
ourselves as a result of our own or others' actions.
When we forgive, we free ourselves of holding
onto the pain. What can you forgive yourself for
that will provide more freedom to live? With
enough compassion the freedom can begin today.

February 12

• • •

Wide, open vista
Pulled forward we come along
It is part of us

With a wider view of our identity we see that loving others and loving ourselves is not such a sharp distinction. When we take care of others, we are taking care of a part of our self. When we take care of our self, we are taking care of a part of others.   See the larger connection you have to the world around you and consider how your compassion makes it stronger.

February 13

• • •

Peaceful and quiet
Drop hanging expectantly
Action releases it

Reflective practices open our eyes to new ways of
seeing things and deeper understanding. They
allow our potential to ripen. Taking the next step,
practicing, transforms potential into reality.
Reflect on compassion often and experiment with
your insights in order to perfect them and make
them real. What growing realization or insight can
you experiment with today?

February 14

• • •

Pain and suffering
It costs nothing to fix it
Now what do you do?

There are times when alleviating suffering costs us nothing. Can this really be true? When we choose not to tailgate the person in front of us, it costs nothing. When we smile at someone, it costs nothing. When we take a deep breath rather than yell at our children, it costs nothing. When we keep a record of all we accomplish each day, it costs nothing. How many others can you think of? Spend five minutes writing down all of the examples you can think of. If you are having difficulties practicing compassion consider starting with these. See how many of them you can do today (and every day.)

February 15

• • •

Darkened, misshaped glass
Brilliant radiant sunshine
Some of it gets through

Whatever relationship we have with our self invariably affects the relationship we have with others. Like glass, our relationship with our self filters both the light coming in as well as the light going out. If our self-relationship is cloudy and troubled what chance do we have of realizing our full potential or supporting the full potential of others? Find a part of yourself that has been neglected or shunned… If you had the ideal relationship with that part of you, what would it look like? Make that ideal relationship a focus of your attention with whatever actions or thoughts make sense for you.

February 16

• • •

Corners all around
Helpful to see around them
Just not possible

Sometimes we believe we know what we really
cannot. And, we act on that belief with absolute
certainty that we are right. What possibilities do
we close off when we act from that position?
What assumptions are you holding onto that affect
how compassionate you are with others and
yourself? How can you test those assumptions to
see how much truth is in them?

• • •

Huge towering tree
Empty wilderness transformed
Potential made real

Sometimes impatience can be a barrier to staying committed to our vision. A tree doesn't grow overnight nor does it grow if it is not provided with good soil and regular watering. It is the steady application of regular practice that provides the conditions for us to become who we want to be. What is your vision for how you will take care of yourself? What were you like when you started these practices? How have you changed? Take a moment to compare where you were when you started, where you are now, and where you want to be. Take heart from whatever progress you have made and consider that what you do today shapes who you will be in the future.

• • •

**We are with winter
In deepest sleep the world stops
Life begins anew**

If we honor the natural cycles that govern us all we take rest when the time comes. Doing so renews; the beginning is always in the end. Without rest we have no opportunity to be reborn. Make rest, whether a full night of sleep, a quiet moment to regroup, or simply not working on a day off, a priority in your life. Be intentional about finding an opportunity to use rest to your advantage during your day today.

February 19

• • •

Dark abyss looms near
Falling steadily, down… down
We choose our own net

Sometimes we are sorely disappointed and get knocked off kilter. No one knows how deep the fall might be. But there is no need to find out. We make our own net by recognizing that we are here for ourselves. A simple affirmation of support such as, "I will stay with you" can be all we need to recognize that we will be OK. Try this whenever you are feeling small or threatened.

February 20

• • •

Shining source of light
Reaching all it still searches
Cannot be used up

Visualize yourself like a light on hilltop, radiating
compassion for the whole world. Letting it flow
from you endlessly. There is no limit to the
compassion you can offer.

February 21

• • •

Seeds move with the wind
Rooted deep is the shade tree
Which one will you be?

Ideas are often exciting. Like seeds, they are full of potential. When we commit to something that potential has the chance to be realized.   What idea or practice have you tried that you can commit to now? Pick one and make it a daily practice for the next month.

February 22

• • •

Boulder on the ground
Suddenly there it appears
Never seen before

As we become more aware we notice things that we didn't see before. Then we start to see them more and more. As we become more familiar with them, we can do something about them. What are you noticing about how you treat or support yourself? What habits have you fallen into that you are starting to notice more often? Keep a log of what you notice for the next week.

• • •

High foreboding walls
A door opens and invites
Now change can happen

When we deny or disown parts of our self we are inherently confirming that we are unworthy. And when we operate from a sense of unworthiness it is very difficult to be our best. One of the greatest acts of self-compassion is to open the door to all of who we are. Especially to those parts we don't always acknowledge and work with. It is only when we accept all of who we are that we can change and become stronger advocates for what is good for us.

Today is Day 2 of the practice.

February 24

• • •

Songbird in a tree
Sweet, melodious chirping
No list is required

We enjoy the sweet sounds of a bird happily chirping in a tree. It brightens our day. For them, it is not a conscious thing. They do this as it is part of their nature. Practicing compassion is like this. As we connect more with others we express compassion as part of who we are, not because it is on our to-do list of things to do. Being intentional in our practice and then expressing what is sincere for us is how we develop our own spontaneous compassionate nature. Being intentional and practicing just to say we did it is not. When being intentional, always connect to a sincere wish or urge before acting.

Today is day 3 of the practice.

• • •

**Dewdrop hangs so low
Bullfrog crouches by the pond
Not a thing happens**

Sometimes our compassion is defined by what doesn't happen. When we support ourselves by choosing differently in the face of old habits it is the dawn of a new life. This is how we build the life we want for our self.

Today is day 4 of the practice.

February 26

• • •

North star in the sky
Uncertain steps plod ahead
Where are you going?

The motivation to take a journey requires more than knowing the general direction. Just as leaving something unpleasant provides motivation, so does going to a destination that we want to reach. The more we can describe and picture who we want to be and how we want our lives to be, the more we can rely on this to motivate ourselves to take the steps to get there. A clear vision of our best self is like a beacon that draws us forward, encouraging us to support our self. It helps us take the sometimes difficult steps that will make us into who we want to be.

What is your vision of a more compassionate life? What will you feel like, how will you experience the world when you protect and care for yourself. How will others benefit when you are that person? Take 10 minutes out today and write down all you can to describe what that life is like.

Today is day 5 of the practice.

February 27

• • •

Three pigs with houses
Large wind comes to blow them down
One remains standing

When we have a vision of our better self and strengthen it, it stands a better chance of becoming reality. By not just thinking about who we will be but also physically and emotionally sensing how we will feel when we are that person, we give our vision the strength it needs to survive. The more we can ground ourselves in how we will be, the more we can actually believe we are capable of it. And the more we believe we are capable, the more likely our vision will endure and become real.

Today is day 6 of the practice.

• • •

The bowl stands ready
It holds all of who we are
Do we dare fill it?

Accepting all of our self, not just who we are comfortable with, is a true act of self-love. Anything we exclude literally prevents us from being whole. This includes the parts we may not like so much but equally includes the gifts we have but deny or discount. Sometimes our gifts are harder to own and accept than the parts we don't like. How much more would you risk and accomplish if you fully used all of your talents? How much more would others benefit?

What are the gifts that you have been denying or discounting? Own them and find some small ways to start using them more often.

Today is day 7 of the practice.

February 29

• • •

Big rocks stand silent
Raindrops bring life to the plants
Day-to-day moments

Most of life is lived in everyday events, not in the grand moments. Appreciate these as opportunities to bring compassion more readily into your life. When we can bring compassion into the small, everyday, ordinary moments of our life we will have lives filled with compassion. If we only look for big, dramatic opportunities we will miss most of the life we live. Keep a count today of how many really small opportunities to be kind to yourself and others you find.

March

March 1

• • •

**Toddler by the chair
Down and up, down and up, down…
Practice makes perfect**

Learning to be self-compassionate, and having a
natural inclination to supporting others, is a trait
that is strengthened through practice. Each time
we fail is a chance to get back up and try again.
Trying again is the sign that we are succeeding. As
with all things we experience, practice is how we
get better. One day we find we no longer have to
think about it. It just happens. Celebrate every
time you come back to the practice as a victory.

March 2

• • •

One step at a time
Home off on the distant ridge
We do what we can

Sometimes we see ourselves falling short of the mark. We know we are not where we want to be. Perhaps we just aren't able to get there at this time. In times like this we have a chance to be compassionate with our self. We can recognize that we are doing what we can and leave it at that, knowing that with each step we will continue to get closer. Try letting yourself off the hook when you are disappointed in your own actions. Instead, resolve to continue to work at it, knowing that that is what will carry you to your goal.

• • •

River tumbling down
Stepping out, all is so calm
Ready to jump in

Taking a brief pause to gain perspective can interrupt the jumble of feelings or judgments that we at times experience. Sometimes it is all we need to re-establish a calm connection with ourselves to see things more clearly. When that happens we can make good decisions and avoid creating more difficulty or suffering for ourselves. When you notice that you are turning on yourself or having harsh judgments of others, consciously step back, become more aware of the present moment, check your feelings against what is true, and then make a choice that serves you well. Practice noticing when you are distressed, and then taking a short pause to become more present and grounded.

March 4

• • •

Tilling the garden
Working the old soil is hard
Ah, to see it grow!

Sometimes we get tired and burnt out trying so hard to be a certain way. This is especially true when we lose sight of the goal and focus on the work. Let the joy of envisioning how you want to be be your motivation today.

March 5

• • •

Flowers in the field
Majestic, they need nothing
They can be enjoyed

When things are going well they should simply be enjoyed. Allow yourself the pleasure of simply admiring the good you see in yourself and others. Just enjoy, nothing else is needed or helpful.

March 6

Day-to-day living
Tucked inside every moment
Opportunity

The more we use our compassion the stronger it becomes. Therefore, noticing how we can offer compassion in all of the small moments of our daily life is a tremendous opportunity to grow. Be alert to these opportunities always. When you are not, simply return your attention back to seeing them.

• • •

Feather in the wind
Wind picks it up and holds it
Small thing but great joy

Throughout the day we have many opportunities to compliment and affirm ourselves: the good decisions we make, the keeping of commitments, the support we offer others. Small things are often what give us great joy. Why not celebrate what you do well and savor the moment of joy that results?

• • •

**Two strangers passing
In a brief moment, smiles flash
Joy begins for both**

Can there be many things easier to do than to look someone in the eye and smile at them? It may be the simplest way to treat yourself and others to a joyful experience. Try it with five strangers today and notice how you it lifts your spirits and how it impacts others.

March 9

• • •

Looking to connect
Hearts reaching out and open
Waiting, always there

Visualize your own heart opening and reaching out to the hearts of others and hold the door of acceptance and caring open for them. Your mind and behaviors will follow. Try this with everyone you meet with today.

• • •

Small room to work in
Stepping outside takes courage
Allows room to grow

When we support and love ourselves, we can drop our old habits of self-judgment. The small confines of limited possibilities then drop away. Suddenly a much larger and richer world is there. Stepping out of those familiar confines requires courage and is an act of self-compassion.

What limiting beliefs about yourself keep you from doing more? Pick one and write down what new possibilities could become available to you when you can stand by yourself and find the courage to walk into that new space.

March 11

• • •

Warm waters, soft light
Sensuous waves lap the shore
Let all of it in

Breathe deep and luxuriate in the love you naturally have for yourself. Appreciate in your heart the small victories you win with every act of self-care and compassion. What are all the small and bigger ways that you have taken care of yourself? Find all of those moments that you can today. Appreciate each one as you notice or remember it.

• • •

Two halves of a stream
Run now in separate ways
Both are made weaker

Anger towards another can split us apart. When we compassionately consider what is driving the other party to act the way they are, we can understand how their behavior makes sense to them. Doing so allows us to escape the further wounding of ourselves from the negative stories we would otherwise tell ourselves. Thus, when we exercise compassion towards another we are being self-compassionate as well. Seek to understand how you can help the other party heal before you respond.

共感

• • •

Stones, some sharp, some smooth
One becomes like the other
Compassion wears smooth

Force and violence can splinter a rock into a form with sharp edges. Steady wearing from natural forces softens the edges to create the smooth beautiful shapes we find in the desert or riverbeds or mountain summits. Today's practice is to hold that image in your heart and to recognize how your own sharp edges have begun to smooth out with the steady contemplation and practice of compassion.

March 14

• • •

Frigid air and ice
Clouds part and sun shines above
The snow slowly melts

Patience allows compassion to do its work. See how often you can pause and stay present with your own suffering or that of another. An open heart that continues to wait with love can outlast and overcome the pain. Make regular practice of this patient, loving stance part of your every day routine.

March 15

• • •

Beauty in full view
We walk by not seeing it
OK to return

There are times when we have an opportunity to
express or receive compassion and we miss it.
Later, we can experience regret when we realize
what we passed by. If we lack self-compassion we
can get caught in a loop of self-recrimination. A
compassionate response is to take steps to return
to the situation and then let the wisdom of your
heart act.

• • •

Mama bear with cubs
Rears mightily when threatened
Love keeps her guard up

Self-compassion motivates us to protect ourselves in the same way that a mama bear protects her cubs. A mama bear's natural aggression can also be seen as compassion for her offspring by protecting them from mortal danger. In the same way, developing compassion for ourselves is what gives us the spine to say "no" to what hurts us. When we practice compassion, we protect our boundaries not as an attack on others but as an act of love to protect ourselves. What boundaries can you strengthen by saying, "yes" to yourself more often?

共感

March 17

• • •

The three little pigs
Big, bad wolf has bad intent
Third pig gives lesson

Compassion is more than relieving pain or suffering. It is also taking steps to avoid pain and suffering. When we care for ourselves by becoming more self-reliant, more skilled, and stronger, we are exercising our self-compassion. In the process we create more capacity to be of service to others. What new skill or capability can you develop to become more self-reliant? At the end of the day write down the skill and the first step you have taken to develop it.

Now make a note on your calendar one month, two months, and three months out to check the status of your progress in developing this new skill.

• • •

Twinkling eyes, wry smile
Unchained spirit soars skyward
Self-love is freedom

When we fully accept who we are, and take steps
to protect and strengthen our self, we find that we
are free. Create and feel that vision of yourself
whenever you are challenged in your practice.

March 19

• • •

Lurker just in sight
Heart pounding, stay on the move
Relief to find self

When we avoid any part of our self it is always still there, still with us. We can ignore it, deny it, run from it. But it is still there, just at the edge of our consciousness. What a relief to accept all of who we are and become whole. What parts of yourself are you dimly aware of that you have been hiding from? Carl Jung was quoted as saying; "We cannot change anything until we accept it." Accepting that which we have been running from is the first step to changing it. And, once we accept all of our self, we become, by definition, whole.

March 20

• • •

Starry sky at night
Full moon passes overhead
Daytime once again

Today is the vernal equinox (at least in the
northern hemisphere), when day and night are
closest to being of equal length during the year.
Let this natural cycle be a metaphor for even-
handedness and equanimity. Being able to
experience life's ups and downs with equal
acceptance serves as a foundation for your
compassion. Be kind to yourself and make
equanimity your practice today – recognizing that
what is true today will be different tomorrow – and
tempering your response accordingly.

共感

March 21

• • •

Dreamy fantasy
Brought down to earth everyday
Solid and unseen

Sometimes we imagine and project so much onto
self-compassion that it becomes unreal, something
that can only be aspired to. Yet when we practice
it everyday we find it is better than that, it is
practical and natural and supportive of a stronger,
better us. Celebrate your continued practice and
the many ways it uplifts your spirit and your life.

• • •

Large gong is struck true
Sound vibrates across the land
Harmony is truth

What is it that is true about the times when compassion comes more naturally than others? Consider what it is you are focused on. When we love ourselves without condition it is easier to be self-compassionate than when we are working to protect a false identity. Likewise, when we are focused on simply wanting others to suffer less, without an agenda or wanting something in return, compassion is natural.   Use today to notice how you are relating to yourself and to others. What is the truth that underlies it? How does that compare to your experience of the compassion you are expressing?

March 23

• • •

Newborn wanders off
Mother brings her back, again
Quick, before she's lost!

Enforcing boundaries early can sometimes feel
hard, like we are being the bad guy. But when the
boundaries are there to support wellbeing and
prevent difficulty, we are being the opposite of
compassionate if we let them slide. Being
compassionate doesn't mean we feel all soft and
warm, sometimes it feels uncomfortable and hard.
Where in your life would you and others benefit
from you being "tougher?"

• • •

Winds blow steadily
Highest tree is standing tall
Safety in deep roots

As we stand up for our self and support our self with love and compassion we strengthen our ability to withstand the challenges that come with life. Self-compassion is not something soft and mushy, it is what builds strength, longevity, and capacity to do good in this world. Take five minutes and list the things you could achieve with a stronger foundation beneath you.

March 25

• • •

Raindrops from the sky
On earth they join together
The river flows on

Compassion is not a grand event although it is
grand. Nor does it need to be dramatic, although
its impact can be. We live our lives in moments.
Each one offers a way to live compassionately, a
way to alleviate suffering, a way to nourish. Simple
acts with good intent. One by one they accumulate
and their impact is multiplied. In what simple ways
can you avoid creating suffering today, for others
and for yourself? Keep this in mind and let it guide
you all day.

• • •

Spring after winter
Thaw shows possibility
All as it should be

As we practice every day we begin to see signs of growth and new strength invigorating us. It carries us a little further each day until we look back and realize we have changed. Let the recognition of your progress be your practice today.

March 27

• • •

Children growing up
Demanding, resistant, hard
We choose to love them

Some things in life are hard but we keep doing them anyhow. The payoff may not be there at that moment but, deep inside, we know it is the right thing to do. Practicing compassion can be like this. We don't do it because it is easy. We don't stop because it is hard. We do it because we know that we, and the world at large, are better off for it. Consider who you will be if you don't make the effort to practice compassion with yourself and others. Consider who you are becoming and will become as you practice compassion more. How will this affect the world around you?

March 28

• • •

Fat caterpillars
Hard winter challenges all
Clues all around us

Sometimes we look back and see we created stress for others and ourselves when it could have been avoided. If we pay attention to these situations we will usually find some clues that precede these actions. Recently I missed an opportunity to empathize with my wife when she was experiencing some emotional stress. Later I couldn't believe how insensitive I had been. When I examined that and similar situations I realized that I had a clear tightening in my solar plexus just before I missed my chance to empathize. That physical sensation was my clue. By paying attention to it I had a tip-off that I might be losing my connection to the present reality, and a chance to course correct before it was too late.

Everyone has their own clues, most often they show up in the body; sometimes they are experienced as a state of mind. Finding your own clues is a key to breaking through old patterns that might be holding you back. Start noticing your own behavior and find the clues that precede the actions you would like to change.

March 29

Hungry souls waiting
Food is free and there to give
What will happen next?

Essentially this is the choice we face. Everywhere
we turn there is a need that compassion can fill. It
costs us nothing to give and is always available.
What will happen next? Think about this question
and how you want to respond as you go through
the day.

March 30

• • •

**A stick and a rock
Together as a lever
Possibility!**

We limit our selves and others when we see others or ourselves as less than what we can really be. This is a subtle way that we contribute to suffering and harm in the world. We can also fix it. Practice seeing yourself and everyone else as much more than what you reflexively believe. What happens when you do this? What do you notice?

March 31

• • •

Sun breaks through the clouds
Day made brighter, spirits lift
Don't be a poop head!

I guess I gave this one away with the last line. I had to say it. It's about as straightforward a practice as there can be. Why rain on someone's parade or dampen their spirits if it is in your power to brighten their day?

April

April 1

• • •

Bare room is quiet
Searching for relationship
Found myself waiting

When we are alone we are in an ideal position to practice compassion. We sometimes forget that we can always be doing something to support our self. Simple tasks or actions like cleaning our desktop, writing a letter, taking a short walk, reading a book, resting if needed. All can make us feel better or position us for an opportunity or strengthen a skill or keep us healthy or... Make a list of those simple tasks and keep it with you for just such a time. Whether it is 15 minutes or a whole day, we can always be good to ourselves.

共感

April 2

• • •

One pointed focus
Hounds following the trail's scent
Inevitable

When we keep compassion as our focus the result
cannot be in doubt. We suffer less, others suffer
less, we become stronger, and others become
stronger. Perhaps we keep better boundaries for
our self, or conserve our energy for what is
important, or act when it is helpful; the means are
many but the focus is the same. Throughout the
day keep compassion as your focus and see what
ways you discover to support yourself and others.

April 3

• • •

Dawn's daylight rises
Replacing the night's darkness
Both are beautiful

Saying "yes" to what gives you life and strength is
the flip side of saying "no" to what we can't afford
in time, money, or energy. Both are beautiful ways
to support your self. For some, framing your
actions in terms of the "yes" may be more
motivational and inspiring. If this is the case, think
of the life you want to say, "yes" to more often so
that the "no's" you must say are simply a
reinforcement of that.

April 4

• • •

Waves on the water
Some zigging, and then zagging
All reach the shoreline

Does anything move in a straight line? Some days
are just tougher than others and we find we aren't
very good at being compassionate. It feels like we
have gone two steps back and we wonder if we are
really making any progress. Knowing that life is like
this in so many other ways makes it easier to
accept and carry on as best we can. Continuing to
practice regardless is what will win the day.

April 5

• • •

Stockpile of acorns
Winter lack made easier
Learn from the squirrels?

Sometimes we miss the good we do and get discouraged. When this happens our life can seem barren. Noticing the good things we do, even the smallest of acts, can counteract this vicious cycle. Writing them down reinforces their impact. Having a record serves as our own storehouse of reminders when needed. Start your list today and keep it handy for easy reference.

• • •

Energy for change
We must want to move forward
One step at a time

"We must want to move forward." This is the key,
isn't it? There are two ways we gain momentum.
The first is becoming sick of the pain we are in (this
usually isn't hard...) The second is having a clear
vision of a brighter future. Work on this step
today. Write down five attributes of what a better
you looks and feels like.   Now write down five
attributes of what a better world looks and feels
like when you relate to the world with compassion.

April 7

• • •

Today is rainy
Yesterday was cold with sleet
Better than before

Whatever kind of day you are having you will have
many moments of choice. With each one you have
an opportunity to respond in different ways. Every
time you make a choice that is more
compassionate than your first instinct, you make
progress in your practice.   Make being better, not
perfect, your focus today. Your chances for success
will be much greater and your capacity for
compassion will grow as a result of steady
progress.

• • •

Lovers and dear ones
Sharing freely unites them
This is true for you

We spend more time with ourselves than in any other relationship. And while it may seem odd to consider a relationship with our self, we experience this all the time. As an example, how often do you judge yourself? So, what can we learn from great relationships to improve the one we have with our self? Deep, enduring relationships feature intimate sharing. We are all probably familiar with the letter writing that went on between great lovers and friends of the past (and continues with some today.) What would you write to yourself as your own best friend? Take 15 minutes today to write a letter from a future, wiser you to your current self. Write to yourself as if you were addressing a dear friend and offering them your sincere appreciation for who they are and your best guidance.

April 9

• • •

Days pass without food
Hungry wolves are on the prowl
Think of just one thing

How can we serve others if we neglect our own
basic needs? When we are less than whole we are
less likely to be in a position to help others or
ourselves. What would it mean if you accepted
your experience of joy or owned your shortcomings
or claimed your own opinions as valid on their
own? What if you were whole and complete and
not disowning any part of yourself? How much
more confident and powerful would you be?
Today, take the time to accept what you might
otherwise deny. Let it soak in if it is joyful or
pleasant. If it is something you aren't satisfied
with, examine it and get to know it, and then take
steps to correct it. Tonight, write down what you
learned and what you plan to do differently as a
result.

April 10

• • •

Four-legged creature
Sharp teeth, foul breath, set to spring
Puppy wants to play

Compassion starts when we wish the best for others and ourselves. Yet we can be quick to judge and miss the reality of others. We can even unfairly judge ourselves. As you go about your day today, notice how often you add your own interpretations to those around you. When you notice this happening, remind yourself of what you do know and start from there.

April 11

Trained rat in a maze
It can always find the cheese
What is it missing?

Sometimes we feel like we have to do certain
things, even when they aren't what we really want
for ourselves. Yet, we've gotten so good at it we
keep doing it. It's easy, we know how to do it, and
we're good at it. But it isn't nourishing us and we
feel empty. What if we learned that we are under
no obligation to do what's "expected" of us? What
would you do differently? What would you create
for yourself? What new gifts might you offer the
world? Consider that throughout the day and
record your reflections before the day ends.

• • •

**Doorway stands ready
At its threshold we are poised
Walking through feels good**

Sometime today you will likely find at least one
opportunity to do something for someone that will
help him or her, something that causes no harm to
you. Notice any resistance you might have. If it is
there, stop whatever you are doing and take the
opportunity anyhow. See how it changes your
outlook and your day. Later, examine your
resistance to the actual experience.

• • •

Doorway stands ready
At its threshold we are poised
Shutting door feels good

Sometime soon you will likely find at least one
opportunity to do something for someone that will
help him or her, something that will come at your
expense, in either time, stress, or other scarce
resources. If you say, "yes" to that opportunity
what will you be saying, "no" to? If you say, "no"
to it, what will you be saying, "yes" to? Knowing
our boundaries, and what it is we are defending,
are keys to exercising self-compassion that keeps
us healthy. What is it you want to say, "yes" to in
your life? What can you say, "no" to in order to
make more room for it?

April 14

• • •

A perfect spring day
Leaves turn slowly with the sun
Appreciation

When we have accepted who we are as whole and worthy we have no need to compare ourselves to others. This allows us to appreciate others for who they are and to see the unique gifts they bring to our experience. Humility is the result. Put away your yardstick of others for a day. See them as neither higher nor lower than yourself. Notice what learning or insight they offer you that you might not have seen before.

April 15

• • •

Chipped paint, sagging roof
Inside warmth and love is found
Perception is flawed

What we see in others is rarely more than a surface glimpse of a much more complex picture. Our judgments fail to account for what we do not see. We might think and act differently towards them if we knew what lay behind their behaviors and actions. Henry Wadsworth Longfellow may have said it best when he penned, *"If we could read the secret history of our enemies, we should find in each man's life sorrow and suffering enough to disarm all hostility."*

When faced with bad behavior from others consider what in their secret history might account for their actions before you respond. Defend your own wellbeing but also consider how you can avoid detracting from theirs. By opening your heart to the possibility of his or her own secret history you may find this easier to do.

• • •

Difficult challenge
No results but still trying
Resolve is strengthened

As hard as we try and as much as we want to be compassionate there are those times where it escapes us. Even while watching ourselves and knowing that we are failing we try anyhow. This is not all bad. We have the right intent, by trying anyhow we likely avoid some of our worst excesses, and we learn more about how to work with ourselves. Best of all, our resolve to continue to expand our compassion is exercised and keeps us on the path.

• • •

Smile crosses my lips
And now ripples on and on
Opportunity!

The chance to show compassion exists in everyday moments. Consider the simple act of smiling. A smile invariably makes us feel better and almost everyone smiles in return. How much better do you feel when you smile at others and genuinely wish them well (even when it is silent)? How much good might you generate when they, in turn, feel a little lighter, even if for a moment? Some will carry that brief sense of joy and appreciation to others and a chain reaction starts. All from a simple smile. Find those moments today where you can express compassion in small ways: a smile, a wave, a kind word and engage your entire day with a compassionate heart.

Note: It has been one month since you were invited to work on a new skill. What can you do now to accelerate or maintain the progress you have made (or start anew)?

April 18

• • •

Untamed animals
Behaving predictably
No magic needed

Rewarding actions produces more of them. No news there. We see it everywhere in our lives, in nature, in business, in politics. What do we want more of in ourselves? How much better off would we be if we rewarded ourselves for doing what supports a healthier experience of life? Name three or more ways you can reward yourself whenever you notice yourself doing something in support of yourself. Start using them today.

April 19

• • •

**Doing, not thinking
Across the sky geese fly north
No longer stuck**

We can turn ideas over in our mind and contemplate with the best of them. And it can feel good. At least for a while. Sooner or later we realize we're stuck. Before you know it, we might even be criticizing ourselves. That's a far cry from putting ourselves in a position to suffer less! The answer, of course, is to shift to doing. Even the smallest step creates more change than the grandest thought.

April 20

• • •

The sun is shining
Clouds move in across the sky
Where is the sun now?

Regardless of what we believe about our capacity
for compassion, it is always there. Knowing that
can help us recognize the importance of removing
what is getting in the way. What gets in the way
when you find yourself not practicing compassion?
Take a moment to record what comes to mind.
Pick one to be mindful of and see how you can let it
go or overcome it.

• • •

Stiff, strong, relentless
Winds blow, we refuse to bend
Now it is too late

Have you ever had the experience of being in an argument and knowing you were wrong? Or at least knowing you were over-reaching, or being more obstinate or cold than what would be helpful? Well, I have. As my positioned hardened and I convinced myself of my righteousness, I missed opportunities to empathize. I also missed opportunities to reduce the pain of the argument. When you find yourself hardening your position, pause and step back. Ask yourself if there is a mistake you are making. Accepting it will be the key to reducing your own and the other party's immediate and lingering distress.

• • •

Weak, tired, bruised, hungry
Our heart goes out to others
We know well that pain

When we react to how others are acting we are responding to what we see on the surface. What if we knew the person had just been fired, or lost a friend, or not slept in days or hadn't had a square meal in weeks? Odds are we'd stand a better chance of empathizing and our reaction would be more compassionate. Pema Chodron made popular the saying, "Just like me, this person…" You can fill in the sentence with whatever you like that helps explain why someone might be acting the way they are. Try it and see if how it affects your ability to respond compassionately.

April 23

• • •

A blustery day
Leaves scatter and wind whistles
How unlike stillness

Taking a short pause to settle is like the change we notice when the wind dies down in the midst of a blustery day. The noise in the trees stops, old leaves lay silent on the ground, and it seems like all of our other senses are heightened. We can experience the same thing when we intentionally choose to pause and allow ourselves to rest in the stillness inside us. We become more centered and grounded and make clearer choices for ourselves. Pick some times today where you will stop, step back, and put yourself in touch with what is important.

• • •

A doozy first flight
Momma bird knows what is best
A push from the nest

Not everything comes naturally. Our first attempts
are often awkward and uncomfortable. But after
we take them it gets easier and eventually it
becomes natural. All because we crossed the line
and made those early attempts. Sometimes,
however, we need a little extra oomph to make
that first step happen. If expressing compassion
requires a push consider who or what can help. A
friend to hold you accountable? A modest
challenge to experiment with? A role model to
emulate? A clear vision of how life will change for
the better? Lock in that source of extra strength to
make those challenging steps easier.

April 25

• • •

Tranquil and flowing
A river follows its banks
Not unusual

By following our practices repeatedly compassion becomes just what is natural. Appreciate those days. Let that river flow.

• • •

Tired, hungry, needy
Now rested, content, strengthened
True friends to ourselves

Being compassionate with our self is the
prerequisite to being compassionate for others.
Everyday we have opportunities to practice this.
We start with the basics. When tired, we rest.
When hungry, we nourish ourselves with good
food. When in need, we find ways to satisfy our
lack. Sometimes we succeed; sometimes we miss
the mark. But we try nonetheless because that is
what friends do. Let your self take care of your self
by taking an action that is important to your
wellbeing. Pick a single item and make it a habit
everyday for the next three weeks. Make a record
of it and follow your progress.

• • •

A good deed is done
Pay it forward to your self
Virtuous circle

Self-compassion includes allowing ourselves to experience the positive sense of satisfaction when we practice compassion. When we allow ourselves to experience positive feelings for what we do well, we become stronger and more likely to continue to express compassion. See how many times you can remember to congratulate yourself for exercising an act of compassion – including the small ones.

• • •

Trampled and beat up
Heavy weights press down on us
Love yourself and rest

There are days when the weight of all that has gone wrong works to drag us down physically, mentally, and emotionally. Pushing to stand up for our selves can feel like even more work and adds to the weight. If you find yourself in that situation, love yourself. Take a different tack and take a rest from the negative. Simply dwell on the knowledge that nothing about you has changed. You are still worthy of happiness. Appreciate yourself. And rest as needed, on all levels.

April 29

• • •

Garden so well kept
We labor furiously...
While ours is in weeds

What tasks have you taken on that serve others but at your expense? If we look around we may find more than we realize. Sometimes we've taken on the task under the assumption that it is our responsibility when actually it is not. This can happen easily with emotions. We're all familiar with tiptoeing around an issue that you fear will upset someone else. When these come at the cost of your own wellbeing it is time to recognize that the responsibility for these emotions belongs to the other party. They are not our burdens to bear. Look around and write down one example of how you have taken on someone else's work. What are the steps you need to take to free yourself of this situation. Write out your thoughts on this today and start putting them into action.

• • •

Obsession beckons
Another voice is followed
Habits come apart

Having self-compassion starts with intention. But that only gets us so far. Sooner or later the strength of our well worn habits take over. We find ourselves doing things because it is what we always have done. We feel compelled to follow that. When we hear a different voice calling we can choose to follow it. Being clear about where that new voice leads helps us take action. Let the pull of a more compassionate life lead you to new ways of being and let old habits come apart. Name five things a more compassionate life will bring and visualize how life will be when they are real.

May

May 1

• • •

Trees in the forest
One falls when no one is near
Noise? Who cares? It falls

We can ease suffering or prevent it in silence, when no one is watching. It can be entirely private or anonymous. It can be as simple as moving something from a walkway that people might trip on or cleaning up a run down area or shoveling a neighbor's driveway when they are sick. Perhaps it is an extra measure of care so that your customer will have a better experience. Our intention and our actions is what matters. How many new opportunities to practice compassion does this open up for you? Jot down your ideas now and see what possibilities present themselves to you.

• • •

Giant waves at sea
Chaotically crashing
Calm at a distance

Perspective changes what we see and what we experience. It's the same event but how it affects us is different. Remembering this, we can use the power of a new perspective to restore our balance. There are many ways we can shift perspective. A pause is a simple one that we examined before. And there are others. We can shift our perspective of time ("How will I think about this tomorrow, or in six months, or a year from now?") We can shift our perspective of person ("If I were my Great Aunt/mentor/spiritual hero/best friend/most admired businessman how would I handle this?) We can shift our perspective of knowledge ("What facts could change how I think about this?") You may come up with others of your own. Pick a situation where you know you are challenged in your ability to be compassionate and try shifting your perspective.

May 3

• • •

Strangers surround us
We freely offer our gifts
Warm feelings abound

Compassion thrives when we express our good will
freely and assume the best of others. When we
extend kindness easily and without condition it is
most often received warmly and a virtuous cycle
can begin. Try this in a situation today where you
do not know others.

• • •

Open and present
All around crosscurrents swirl
Discernment maintained

In the midst of turmoil we can keep our heads
when we stay open and present to what we are
experiencing. Open in the sense of not judging or
foreclosing possibilities. Present in the sense of
being aware of what is happening as it happens.
This ability to stay involved but not attached allows
us to see what is most important and make choices
that help support our own wellbeing and that of
others. How do we develop this capacity?
Meditation is one technique used by many for
millennia. Find a resource for learning and
practicing and make it a daily habit, even if only for
a few minutes a day. It will become easier and
more natural as you continue in your practice.

• • •

Water in the ground
Leaves rise up taking it in
Roots are important

There is a great deal of good in all of us. When we appreciate it we become stronger and steadier. Connecting with that goodness is an act of self-compassion. This requires us to both recognize the good in us and to accept it. One way to do this is to both notice and record the good in you each time it surfaces. No amount of goodness is too small to note. Both quantity and quality matter. A notebook and a pen or other device is all you need. At the end of each day review what you've captured. Make this a practice for the next week.

May 6

• • •

Frenetic noises
Seventy-eight RPM
Meant for thirty-three

OK, this is a challenge haiku for most anyone born before 1965 perhaps? A quick history lesson: when vinyl was the medium of choice for audio recordings there were different playback speeds. Playing a recording at the wrong speed resulted in distorted sounds. The lesson of this haiku? Sometimes we have to slow down to understand what is really going on. Doing so brings about greater clarity and better choices as a result. How can you slow down today in your interactions and thoughts? Practice and experiment with the ideas you come up with.

Today is day 2 of the practice.

May 7

• • •

Silent skies above
Tranquil water lays smooth… flat
Fierce screams now empty

What isn't present defines what is. When we refrain from negative thoughts, habits, and behaviors we find a very different world. Choose something negative to let go off today and see how your experience changes.

Today is day 3 of the practice.

May 8

• • •

Feathered nest soft, warm
Momma bird flies to and fro
Cradle for new life

Nests are built one twig, one feather, one stalk of straw at a time. Eventually the nest takes shape and new life has a home. It is through repeated intentional efforts that conditions for creating new life develop. And so it is with our practices to develop compassion. An intentional focus is what allows us to develop our capacity and to keep building it. Choose an area of practice that you want to be intentional about and stick to it today. You may want to review some of your past exercises for ideas or choose a new one.

Today is day 4 of the practice.

May 9

• • •

Flowers face sunward
Turning to gather the light
Nothing else needed

It is amazing how well things go when we do what we need to do. Being intentional in our actions in support of ourselves is a powerful self-compassion practice. Not only does it nourish us, but it avoids the drain of energy from errors and neglect. For some, simply making a to-do list in the morning and sticking to it can have a huge impact. For others, it may be aligning our actions with our purpose more effectively. For still others it may be getting clear about goals and creating milestones to work towards. Or maybe all three! Start simple, start where you are, and create a means of systematically attending to the important things in your life.

Today is day 5 of the practice.

• • •

The plant and the sun
Irresistible movement
Authentic living

Moving naturally in the world is a far kinder way to live our lives than forcing ourselves to be something we are not. How can we live in a way that is as natural as a plant following the sun? Purpose is what attracts us and lifts us and following it makes life simpler and more satisfying. What could be more self-compassionate than living the life that rewards your basic instincts and motivations? How do we know our purpose? Paying attention to what lies at our core, what gifts we have to offer, what draws us forward, what engages us in a way that comes from the inside are all clues. Spend time increasing your awareness of these things. Write down what you notice in a place you will revisit and refine.

Today is day 6 of the practice.

May 11

• • •

Rainbow bright and clear
The sky is made majestic
Our spirits lift up

Inspiration is a wonderful thing. In a moment we can be transformed in our outlook and actions. What inspires you to offer greater compassion to yourself and to the world?

Today is day 7 of the practice.

• • •

Poised, alert, thoughtful
Perspective shifts with insight
No longer the same

When we listen carefully to others we provide
them with respect and both parties benefit. Paying
attention and letting others complete what they
have to say allows us to pause our own reactions.
We learn more about what is important to them.
We also reduce their anxiety about not being
heard. We, in turn, develop patience and
understanding. We have a chance to better
consider our own views and change how we
experience others and ourselves.

May 13

• • •

Quiet plip... plip... plip...
Water dripping slowly down
Stalagmites appear

Little by little we change and grow. Over time the
changes are obvious but in the moment it is
imperceptible. Growing compassion for others and
ourselves is like this. As we continue our practice
we start to see small, subtle shifts. One day we
notice a compassionate reaction we have that is
unlike our prior self.   What small changes have you
noticed? Watch for them today.

• • •

Fog, mist, and shadows
We arm as they move closer
Compassion disarms

The next time you sense yourself tensing up around someone or telling yourself a story about what a jerk someone is or how so-and-so is probably going to screw you, try disarming your negative thoughts with a compassionate response. It can be as simple as saying, "hello" and starting a light conversation – or reminding yourself that they are just like you with their own challenges and foibles. See what kind of changes you experience and how the situation changes.

May 15

• • •

Stark, silent houses
Doors ready to be opened
Warmth and light inside

When we step through the doors open to us we
find a different world inside. This is a key to
compassion, recognizing the inner warmth and
humanity inside each of us and then connecting
with it. Sometimes we have to get past an exterior
that belies that fact. Visualize a warm and feeling
person inside those around you. Focus only on
that sensation. Then let your heart sense connect
with that. Do it again and again until you feel
yourself soften.

May 16

• • •

Boats anchored offshore
Flames rage and they are no more
Commitment now high

We have all probably had the experience of making greater progress when there is no easy way to turn back. How might a commitment to a daily practice of compassion allow you to make greater progress? What can you do to make it more difficult to turn back? How can you create more accountability to help yourself follow through? Answer these questions and then put a plan into place to make your progress more likely.

May 17

• • •

Moon, tides, sun, seasons
Cycles and rhythms surround
Wisdom to be gained

If we ignore what is happening with ourselves we are likely to suffer needlessly. Pay attention to your body and the wisdom it holds. Is it tired and low on energy, is it tight, loose, refreshed and supple, in pain, raring to go? Sleep when tired, rest when injured, act when ready are all simple ways to show compassion for yourself. What is your body telling you today and how can you respond compassionately?

Note: It has been two months since you were invited to work on a new skill. If you have not started, you can today. If you have started, what can you do now to maintain and solidify the progress you have made?

• • •

**Discomforting life
Visions of what could be call
Contrast motivates**

It can be easy to sense and feel the discomfort that we live with. On the other hand, we don't always see the possibilities of what could be if our capacity for compassion was greater. When we can clearly contrast the two extremes, where we are and where we want to be, we develop energy for change. And that energy can help accelerate and ensure our progress. How clearly can you see what life would hold if your compassion was fully developed? What would be different in your life? Reflect on this and sharpen your vision of how your life will change as your compassion grows.

May 19

• • •

Coal mine canaries
The moment of choice foretold
Who would ignore them?

We always reach a crossroads, the last moment when choice is still possible. Sometimes we don't notice it. When that happens we realize, too late, that we acted badly and hurt others or ourselves or maybe both. Other times, we are fortunate and we see that moment as it is about to happen. When we do we can pause and make a choice that promotes wellbeing. The difference between seeing the moment and missing it, is to become aware of the signals that tell us that the crossroads is near. Like a canary in the coal mine we can see trouble before it is too late. Paying attention to physical symptoms is usually the clue. Perhaps it is a tight jaw, shortness of breath, pursed lips, or a racing heart... you get the idea. These sensations are tip offs that we are headed down a path we will later regret. Learn these signals, pay attention to them, and then use them to act more compassionately when challenged. Start noticing what signals your body sends when you are in the danger zone.

• • •

Cornered and ensnared
We lift the net and slip out
One step brings freedom

Getting some distance from the immediate
pressure of a situation allows so many possibilities.
When we can notice that we are getting bound up
in negative emotions and judgments, we have the
ability to step back and reset. We are then able to
see choices and respond more compassionately.
Sometimes a simple deep breath will do,
sometimes we need to let others know we need
some room. Whatever the action is, it is within our
ability to act. Ask yourself how you can create a
little space for yourself the next time you feel
yourself getting closed in.

May 21

• • •

Ready to attack
Like a fog, dark moods hang low
Glad for tomorrow

When we are in a dark mood we can do our best to see past it. Sometimes this doesn't work. We want to be compassionate but it isn't happening. We feel trapped, smothered by our mood. If we can't get past it, we can remember that it will be different tomorrow. Just this thought alone provides some relief in which to take refuge. Remember that nothing lasts and use that realization to help lessen the grip of your dark mood.

May 22

• • •

Rising hill ahead
One shoulder put to the wheel
Troubles left behind

Compassion isn't always glamorous or accompanied by a glow. Often it is the nitty-gritty work of using of our talents and our will to get things done that avoids suffering in the first place. This is helpful to keep in mind when we are challenged by tasks that serve important purposes but that we are tempted to put off. The compassionate choice is to press ahead. How might you apply this today?

• • •

Light dawn starts the day
Crisp air energizes us
Moved by beginnings

How we approach life sets the tone for all that follows. We all know the difference between what we experience when the day starts on a positive note and when it does not. It is the same with our capacity for compassion. A clear intention to help reduce the suffering in the world increases the likelihood that we will succeed. When we can see what can be, we are motivated to help bring it about. Envision what is possible for you and for each person you meet today and let that be the motivation for your compassion.

May 24

• • •

**Apple on the ground
Burrowing inside, worms eat
Too late to harvest!**

Sometimes we are lucky enough to have a window
of opportunity to repair a rupture in our
relationship with others. Even more fortunate is
when we recognize that opportunity and act on it
while we have the chance! Rather than harden
your position, try softening your heart and use
compassion as your guide to heal any wounds you
left behind. (You can also do this with yourself
when suffering from harsh self-judgment that
leaves you feeling inadequate and flawed.)

May 25

• • •

Seeds planted with care
Rich soil, good rainfall, and sun
Abundant harvest

Part of successfully expanding our capacity for
compassion is creating the right conditions for it to
flourish. Good intentions are like seeds. They are
necessary and are often seen as the starting point.
They contain the potential but they are not enough
on their own. We must supply the right conditions
as well.

Pausing, listening, slowing down, connecting with
others' humanity, healthy acceptance of self, and
maintenance of boundaries have all been
mentioned in prior entries. What leads you to your
successful exercise of compassion? Notice what
conditions are present when you find you are at
your best and note these in your journal.

May 26

• • •

Stormy seas toss
Clear skies on the horizon
Gap crossed by action

When we contrast what can be with what is, action
follows. The greater the contrast, the more action.
For most of us, experiencing and seeing the
suffering in and around us is easy. What can you
do to increase the clarity and fullness of your vision
for a better you and a better world? As that vision
increases your use of compassion will follow.

May 27

• • •

On top of a ledge
The trail leads down and across
Not the only route

Seeing possibilities beyond our expectations opens
a new world of available responses. When faced
with challenges and disappointments it is always
helpful to learn from them. It is also always helpful
to ask if there are other satisfying routes that are
outside our preconceived notions. Could other
outcomes be more valuable or satisfying? What's
obvious is often what we are conditioned to and
comfortable with. How can you challenge yourself
to be open to other avenues that support yourself
or support others?

共感

• • •

Mirror bright and clean
Showing our own reflection
Trapped like Narcissus

What happens when you focus exclusively on yourself in an attempt to increase your happiness? Chances are you notice a certain sense of lack or emptiness. Or perhaps you find yourself getting easily irritated. Have you ever noticed how you feel when you try to create happiness by expecting the world to meet your needs? Try flipping the equation around and see what difference you notice.

Note: Do not confuse an exclusive focus on yourself in an effort to boost your own happiness with ensuring your needs are met. Standing up for what is vital to you and caring for yourself is critical to your wellbeing and your ability to help others.

May 29

• • •

Harbor of refuge
Empty and waiting for us
Healing can begin

Self-compassion is always waiting for us when we find ourselves rebuffed and battered. What can keep us from taking refuge in caring for ourselves when we need it? Pride? Anger? Shame? Our self-compassion is always available. One thing that can keep us from it is lack of trying. What would be an act of self-compassion you can practice today that offers some nurturing and healing?

• • •

Long list of to-do's
One-by-one they are knocked down
Day starts to brighten

Self-compassion involves supporting ourselves in ways that reduce the suffering or discomfort we experience. Taking care of business is one way to do this. While it may seem straightforward it implies more than just working diligently. It means making what is important to your wellbeing a priority, it means defending those boundaries that allow you to accomplish those things (saying, "no" to requests that are less vital), it means caring enough about yourself to realize you are worthy of happiness. Finally, for those who feel such behavior is selfish, recognize that a healthier, better you is better equipped to help others!

May 31

• • •

Shiny spider web
A beautiful creation
Many connections

The beauty of a spider web would not exist without
the connections that hold it in place. Compassion
is like this, too.   The elements that support
compassion are also beautiful: an open, caring
heart and wisdom that supports wellbeing. But
without a connection, either with others or
ourselves, compassion remains just a beautiful
concept. As you go about your day, notice when
you are connected and when you are not. Make a
list of ways you can make connection easier.

June

June 1

• • •

Arid, empty field
In the middle, arms outstretched
We accept the rain

What happens when others shower you with warmth? It may be praise, it may be thanks, it may simply be recognition for something you did. Allowing it in and letting yourself soak in it may not be your first inclination. Try it the next chance you get. The exercise of self-compassion includes making ourselves vulnerable to the love around us.

June 2

• • •

Chameleon tries hard
Working to deceive others
Can't be a turtle

When we are not true to ourselves we cannot help others. If we are doing something "good" for appearances, or because it is what we "should" do, it doesn't really help anyone. Certainly not ourselves and certainly not others who often recognize our true intent for what it is. We only have so much time available to us. Use it in ways that honor what is true in your heart.

June 3

• • •

Moments of distress
Anxiety runs rampant
Do it as a gift

We can relieve a great deal of anxiety by shifting how we view our performance. Sometimes we find ourselves judging ourselves and worrying about how others might see us. Instead we can see what we do as a gift for others. Our whole perspective changes when our focus shifts from putting demands on ourselves to supporting others. Try this the next time you find yourself overly stressed by the demands of what you do.

June 4

• • •

Loose sticks all about
Joined together side-by-side
Cannot be broken

Contemplate a world where everyone looks out for everyone else. Where supporting each other is a natural act. It's easy to see what a wonderful world it would be. How can we make this a reality? Certainly we can model the change as individuals. If we are responsible for families or teams or organizations or groups of any size we have even greater possibilities for changing the world for the better. Contemplate that better world frequently and help set the change in motion whatever way you can.

共感

June 5

• • •

What we need ourselves
We often give to others
Are we any less?

The gift we give others may be the one we most
need to receive. What gifts do you give others?
How would it be to receive those? What would
stop you from offering them to yourself? Ponder
these questions today in a deliberate way and lean
into any discomfort you may sense. Know that
self-compassion requires that we believe ourselves
to be worthy of happiness and wellbeing, and that
if we don't have compassion for ourselves we are
limited in what we can offer others.

June 6

• • •

Harsh winds and sun's warmth,
One challenges, one beckons
We stand our own ground

In the face of pressure or temptation we
sometimes say and do things that don't express our
true values and passions. Living as if we are
someone we are not takes a toll on us. When we
act in ways that do not represent who we are, we
are uncomfortable, less confident, perhaps tense,
and often feel less than whole. That's a whole lot
of suffering that can be avoided by speaking and
acting from what is inside us, what we truly believe
and who we truly are. It takes courage to stand
your ground. Self-compassion isn't always easy,
but it is necessary for our wellbeing. Be aware of
when your authenticity is being challenged and see
how your life becomes richer as you learn how to
honor your boundaries.

• • •

Broken down compass
Dispirited traveler
Look up to the stars

Maybe your whole day is falling apart and
compassion is far away. Even worse, you can't
seem to find it or get into a groove. At times like
these remember that you have many tools to find
your way. Slowing down, taking a deep, centering
breath, pausing and seeing alternatives, connecting
with what it might be like to be the other person,
seeking the comfort of a true friend, and many
more are alternatives to try. If one way isn't
working, try another, and invent new ones if you
have to.

June 8

• • •

Shadow passes by
Reflects the bigger picture
What is causing it?

Sometimes a flicker of awareness catches our attention. For a fleeting moment we see something and then we let it go. But if we take a moment to examine it we likely will see something larger at play that called it to our attention in the first place. These moments often offer opportunities to use your compassion to set something right. Notice when you sense, even for a brief moment, that something is tugging at you. Stop and consider the larger reason for that tug. And then choose to act in a way that allows your compassion to make a difference.

共感

June 9

• • •

Big goopy puddle
Waits patiently for our step
Still waiting, bye-bye

Some days are unremarkable when judged by what actually happens. When judged by what didn't happen they are quite remarkable. Never forget that avoiding suffering beats alleviating suffering every time! What goopy puddle in your life will you walk past today?

• • •

**Find out what it means
R.E.S.P.E.C.T.
Take care…TCB**

Ah, if only haiku allowed seven syllables instead of requiring five in the first line! This, of course, is a lift from the iconic song made famous by Aretha Franklin. So, what does it have to do with compassion? When we approach others with respect we are more likely to avoid wrong judgments and the poor choices that come with them. Hence, treating others with respect ultimately leads to less suffering on our part and offers a surprising way to practice of self-compassion.

(In case you are wondering, TCB was 70s slang for, "Taking care of business"… and if you were wondering why seven syllables would have been great for the first line, the words, "to me" are part of the lyrics.)

June 11

• • •

Still, quiet morning
Sun rises and skies lighten
Steady as she goes

Some days go well and it seems like there is no
special need to draw on our compassion. Maybe it
is just coming easily or maybe the challenges are
few. Either way it is still a good idea to always be
watchful for opportunities to support others or
ourselves lest we get lulled into complacency.

June 12

• • •

In the dark river
Tidal flow is pulling us
Stay close to the shore

When temptation calls us and our dark side wants to seek revenge it can be tough to be compassionate. Staying close to our ideals helps reduce the pull. Knowing our negative actions will be the cause of more suffering in the world can keep us from succumbing. Keep your ideals in mind and realize how cause and effect works to avoid adding to the world's troubles. What is your vision for how you want to live in the world?

June 13

• • •

Eyes closed, just darkness
Even fluttering brings light
Truth can become known

When we start noticing our thoughts and
intentions more often, we see more opportunities
to avoid suffering and to support wellbeing.
Noticing them, particularly when they are different
from our aims, helps us spot opportunities to
modify our behavior. So, a practice to try is to
consider a behavior you want to change and start
noticing all you can about it when it occurs. What
you were thinking, what triggered it, who was
involved, etc. Try this and see the impact that
noticing can have on your ability to practice self-
compassion and compassion for others.

June 14

• • •

Lightning can strike here
Troubles happen anywhere
Take care of business

We don't know where the next ordeal will come
from. We don't know when the next problem will
rear its head. We *can* strengthen the hand we
have been dealt. Taking care of what must be
done, and being intentional about our priorities, is
self-compassion at its best. As we strengthen our
position we lessen the impact of the next challenge
to our wellbeing. How well do your priorities
support your growth and your health? How are
you actions aligning with your priorities?

June 15

• • •

Passions deeply stirred
Revenge clouds our compassion
We look for the sun

When we are secure it is easier to be helpful to others. When tested by our hatred, disdain, or dislike for others it is a lot harder. We can balance our temper by considering what we need, and expressing that, instead telling others what they should change. Self-awareness can play a powerful role here. We usually get angry when something important to us isn't happening. By examining what we need, and then making it known, we change the nature of our interaction and avoid the potential for creating even more suffering.

Which approach do you believe will result in less suffering by all involved: Taking shots at others and telling them how you want them to change, or getting in touch with what is important to you and making that known? Take some time to consider who or what is likely to trigger that spark of anger in you. What is it that is important to you that you want them to pay attention to and respect?

June 16

• • •

Quiver of arrows
The archer chooses just one
All fit for the job

There are many avenues for exercising compassion.
Review what you've learned and read and pick an
approach to try at today.

June 17

• • •

Fledglings in the nest
Bumped into flight and awkward
Soaring with practice

Are we any different? Our first attempts at
growing our compassion for others and ourselves is
not automatic and not always graceful. Sometimes
we forget or let ourselves get carried away by old
habits or just lack the motivation. But with
repetition and continued practice we advance
further. The fact that we return to practice time
and again is the clue that we are on the right track.
Celebrate your returning to practice each day
(starting today would be a good idea!)

June 18

• • •

Windows looking out
Mirrors reflecting inward
Compassion both ways

Sometimes we look and look for ways to bring
compassion to others when it is us who need it the
most. Sometimes we focus on ourselves and miss
how we can help others. Both are needed in the
world. Remember each today as you go about
living your life.

June 19

• • •

Rock in the pocket
In the skirmish it stays put
Wounds are avoided

Sometimes when we are angered our first impulse is to strike a decisive blow. When you notice this happening pause for a moment or two and refrain from doing so. Make your point without leveling or harming the other party and you get a double benefit. You'll avoid harming them and you'll likely spare yourself from suffering the reaction that surely would have followed. Being able to pause is one of the most helpful techniques you can develop for staying in control and acting with intention. Practice taking that pause today whenever you notice yourself getting agitated.

• • •

The paved road to hell
Intention doesn't change things
Until we can see

Despite our sincere best interests we must see where others are and what they are ready for when we offer "help." The question to be answered is, 'Who's agenda is it, ours or theirs?" Just because it is a good idea from our perspective doesn't mean it will be helpful for them.   One of greatest acts of compassion is truly and deeply listening to someone, seeing them as they really are, without judgment. Doing this before offering support is a practice that will serve you and others well.

共感

June 21

• • •

The paved road to hell
Intention doesn't change things
We must see ourselves

How well do we really know ourselves, what we
want vs. what we think is right to want? How
much do we notice about what energizes us, what
distracts us, what pulls us into despair, what makes
our life work well? How can we really support our
wellbeing without deeply and fully knowing
ourselves? Start noticing and make notes until you
have a solid list that helps you live your life more
fully. You may want to start with just one item and
develop it before starting another, or you may
want to start with several that call to you most.
Either way, just start.

June 22

• • •

Tire treads on one's back
Make compassion difficult
Speed bumps don't work well

When people run over us it makes it hard to be
compassionate towards them. It really is a simple
truth. We can try to be accepting and sweet but
chances are it won't be how we feel inside. This is
not true compassion. A better answer is to not let
ourselves be run over in the first place. When we
are being run over speed bumps are not enough.
We need barricades. This means saying "no"
whenever saying, "yes" jeopardizes our own health
or important priorities. It means holding others
accountable for their commitments. Compassion
comes from a place of equality, not victimhood or
master. What is an area of your life that you want
to protect and nourish more actively? Who or
what do you need to say, "no" to? What do you
need to do to hold others accountable?

• • •

**Those muddy waters
Clean water is always there
Learn to be, then do**

When we are distracted we don't see things as clearly. Staying busy can be soothing and as we catch glimpses of our own suffering we tend to get even busier. Accomplishment, even the illusion of it (like checking email 20 times a day!), is prized above all else. The problem comes when all that action keeps us from focusing on what our bodies, or emotions, or children, spouses, friends, co-workers, etc. are telling us. The antidote is to slow down. Spend more than a reflexive five or ten seconds letting your feelings and state of being catch up with you. Then make intelligent choices in light of what you see and what your really want for yourself.

June 24

• • •

Mirror turned inward
Shows what we don't want to see
Letting it in helps

When a conversation or interaction doesn't go well
see what you can notice about what drove you to
respond the way you did. Was there a story you
were reacting to, or some past history, or some
darker motivation (like wanting to win or be in
control for its own sake)? The more we can be
aware of our shadow side the more we are able to
respond in healthier ways. Doing so helps us avoid
creating more suffering for others and ourselves.
Being alert for the subtle tracks of what our inner
experience tells us, and acknowledging what is
really there, may not feel good but it can do good.

June 25

• • •

Seeing, not doing
We cower in the shadows
Hollow and empty

Ugh, it's an empty and uncomfortable feeling to know we were wrong but do not own up to it. We can stay there and perhaps no one will know. But we will know. In the meantime we feel awful and the other people don't feel so good either. How do we get out of the trap? When the pain of staying where we are grows larger than the pain of bringing the truth to light we act. Or, when we contrast the pain of where we are with the peace of where we could be we create the energy for change. Either way, dwelling on the suffering we are causing eventually leads us to repair the damage and lets light shine in on the dark places of our life. What painful truths do you glimpse that you quickly push away into the darkness? Hold onto them a little longer before sending them away. Do it again and again until you are able to create the courage to bring them to light and let go of their burden.

• • •

Morning sun rises
Hope becomes reality
Eyes stayed on the prize

Knowing where we want to be is a powerful motivator. By having a clear vision of what we want to change, and keeping it in focus, we are better equipped to take advantage of opportunity. When we can see the benefits of compassion clearly we are more likely to act compassionately. What situation in your life can you try this with today? Where are you stuck in some ongoing suffering? How do you want to act differently? Be clear about what you will do and how you will do it. Be clear about how it will be different when you do that. Then look for an opportunity and practice.

June 27

• • •

Strong or loose rudder
In rough seas the choice is clear
Don't wait for rough seas!

How steady is our own rudder? How strong is our
sense of direction and sense of self? Tending to
our own needs in support of our self makes us
stronger when we need it most. Without this
strength how can we be capable of offering
compassion to others? Choose one thing that will
strengthen you and practice it until it becomes a
daily habit. If necessary, start with the basics:
sleep, solitude, exercise, speaking up, allowing your
light to be seen regardless of what others may
think. Or consider the values that are most
important to you. How will you honor and practice
them? Pick one of these ideas or one of your own
that is calling to you. Find a way to hold yourself
accountable to it each day. Put it on a to-do list, on
a sticky note at your desk, find a friend who will ask
you about your progress, whatever it takes to make
it part of your life.

June 28

• • •

Disjointed living
Compassion is hard to have
Connection needed

When we find little compassion for ourselves or others it may be a sign that we have walled ourselves off. A practice to try out in these circumstances is to connect with others. When we open ourselves to others, compassion naturally follows. It can be as simple as taking a few minutes to genuinely listen to someone. Experiment with finding ways to connect with yourself or others today.

June 29

• • •

In plain view of all
We show ourselves openly
Will it be the truth?

Living a lie takes a toll. Living a half-truth is not much better. Hiding in the shadows can be debilitating. The hard part is that we often do these things in the belief that we are escaping suffering. And perhaps in the short term we succeed. But it eventually catches up with us and we find we are miserable. "This above all: to thine own self be true…" These words from Shakespeare's *Hamlet* are a practice in self-compassion that may be the most powerful we have. Where are you living in ways that are less than authentic? How can you be more true to yourself and your own true story?

• • •

Armies on the field
The front line starts to crumble
Retreat is called for

Carrying on in the face of injury may be noble but there comes a time when getting out of the line of fire is the right thing to do. When you've paused, taken a breath, done whatever you can to avoid getting sucked into a situation you know you will regret, and *still* find yourself in danger, it's time to exit the scene if at all possible. As a last resort, avoiding the creation of, or experience of, more suffering is an act of compassion that likely serves all concerned. Know when you have reached your limits and retreat if needed.

July

July 1

• • •

Staircase stands ready
Always there, waiting for use
Go to your future

Shakyamuni Buddha is credited with saying, "What
you are is who you have been. What you'll be is
what you'll do now." What is the future you want
to create? Consider this carefully as your life
depends on it. Then use today to take the steps
that will lead you there.

• • •

True, false, I don't know
Stories that spin are tested
Avoid loss and pain

If we are pay attention we probably notice that we have a judgment or story about someone based on even the slimmest of evidence. People who wear all black are trying to be cool, or someone who doesn't smile is a bitch, or the well-dressed preppie is selfish, or the person who keeps interrupting just wants to have their way, or whatever… I'm guessing you know what I mean. Testing these stories with a simple, "True, false, or I don't know" often reveals that we don't really know if what we are reacting to is actually true. And with that knowledge we can see and take advantage of more opportunities to connect in a healthy and productive way. Try testing all of your stories as you go through the day.

July 3

• • •

Dark, confused forest
The owl patiently watches
Now all becomes clear

Patience is a virtue. It allows us to be intentional in what we do and avoid mistakes. By taking the time to fully absorb what is around us we can make sense out of confusion and go about our day with greater certainty and less discomfort. Where would a modest amount of patience make your day easier to manage? Experience patience today as your self-compassion practice.

July 4

• • •

Unsettled waters
We do not like what we see
Can we drop anchor?

When we are unsettled and things aren't moving
the way we'd like we have a choice. We can sail
ahead despite the difficulty or we can drop anchor
and take advantage of the delay.   There may be no
way to know which is right. Even worse, we may
be unable to accept that we even have this choice
available to us. If you find yourself feeling uneasy
at the prospect of knocking off or playing when
faced with challenges you may want to understand
what is going on. What's behind the anxiety you
are feeling? Perhaps you will find a "call" – a clear
reason for pressing on. Perhaps you will find a
"dragon" that must be slayed before you can be
comfortable enjoying yourself. Either way, moving
out of indecision will increase your own wellbeing.
This practice is about noticing where you have
indecision and then examining what is behind it so
that you can more confidently move forward.

July 5

• • •

Silent compassion
More than patient listening
Appreciation

Giving the gift of listening is often one of the most helpful things we can do to support another. If we do this out of obligation it loses its impact. When we do it with an attitude of appreciation for the other we not only provide powerful support, our own heart is enlivened and we build our own capacity for compassion. Compassion is more than a checkmark by an activity; it involves feeling another's distress and a desire to help them.   Keep your heart open to others as you practice compassion.

共感

July 6

• • •

Deer in the headlights
The time for action is here
Take steps or perish

Sometimes we can step outside of ourselves and
see our emotions as they unfold. We can see our
anger, our frustration, and our fear developing
right before us and yet we can still be trapped in a
familiar pattern. Seeing our emotions as they take
place gives us an advantage. It puts us in the
position of being able to respond in ways that
reduce negative consequences while we still have a
chance to do so. But if we are like the deer caught
in the headlights, and don't act, we get run over. A
way past this is to be willing to experiment with
changing your pattern and responding differently.
Get in touch with how you want to be and respond
in a way that is more likely to support that vision.

July 7

• • •

A cheery hello
Pulls us from our hazy fog
We can be like that

We can be inspired to compassion by observing it in others. Simply watch others and you will see it happen again and again. Let those acts be inspiration for your own.

• • •

**Riding with the wind
Enjoy the breeze and the view
Enjoying is good**

When things are going well don't look for bad news. Enjoy it.

July 9

• • •

Archer's bow pulled taut
Line of sight joins with target
Intention, then deed

Being intentional about compassion makes it more
likely. That's pretty straightforward. What is
included in intention? Preparation, right tools and
skills, and focus are a good start. How can you
increase your intention?

July 10

• • •

Half empty, half full
Our view changes how we act
What are we missing?

When we see others what do we see? Do we see
their flaws or hold them in a judging view? It is so
easy to spin a story about how someone is without
really knowing anything of substance. What would
it be like if we only saw their strengths? How might
we treat others differently if we approached them
from a level of respect instead of judgment?
Practice looking for strengths or something to be
admired in everyone you meet today.

July 11

• • •

Toddler on her feet
Again and again falls down
But not forever

Pick a practice that is still awkward for you. Now, apply the lessons of a toddler learning to walk. By the time she is few years old walking is natural and easy. In fact, it is hard to imagine it was ever any other way. The same is true of some of our compassion building practices. They don't come naturally and practicing them just once doesn't build proficiency. We have to try them again and again.

July 12

• • •

Alone on a limb
Support is placed under it
No longer alone

Sometimes we think of compassion as making up
for something someone is missing. But sometimes
compassion is providing support to something that
someone is already doing. Adding our voice to
another's can make their journey steadier and their
odds of success that much stronger. We are not
only letting them know we are with them; we are
letting others know as well. Who can you support
in their journey to make a critical difference?

July 13

• • •

Field of bright flowers
Caressing all with their bliss
What could be better?

Savoring our vision of a world where love and
compassion are how lives are lived is a blessing in
and of itself. Fully absorbing that vision, and
experiencing its beauty, is inspirational. Use this to
fuel your desire to help build that better world.

• • •

Moment of choice comes
Freedom is now possible
Do we notice it?

At some level we know when we are about to
cause some harm, either to our self or to others.
When we don't notice that moment, it just goes by
and we fall into our habitual patterns. Perhaps we
get defensive, or angry, or withdraw. What if,
instead, we saw that moment, and broke the cycle
by choosing to respond differently? Choosing to be
more compassionate to our self or others. How
much less suffering would we create? Pay
attention to your habitual reactions and start to
notice when they arise. This practice will allow you
to eventually spot the moment of choice and find
freedom.

July 15

• • •

Lonely unsure path
Stomach and emotions twist
Doing the hard thing

Doing the hard thing is exactly that - hard. Not doing the hard thing, when it is the right thing, isn't so great either. Which leads to less suffering? We know the answer, now we must practice compassion the hard way. Focus on what is important, keep it always foremost in your mind, and then plow ahead.

July 16

• • •

Nose stays just above
Water rising steadily
A lot is at stake!

When tested with strong emotions or difficult
situations we have so much at stake. If we let go
and give up we can suffer or cause so much
damage. Compassion in this situation is
recognizing the danger and simply holding it
together as best we can, avoiding the disaster that
is so close. What do you value most in any given
situation? Would you recognize it if it was in
danger?

July 17

• • •

Rain drop on its own
Potential forever changed
When it meets ocean

It is easy to get trapped into the perspective of "I"
or "me" and forget about the bigger picture. How
do we want to engage as part of the larger world?
What can we offer or support? When we take that
larger perspective our compassion comes more
easily. How do you want to engage the world
today, what do you want to support?

July 18

• • •

Numerous windows
We dart between each, searching...
Choose a pleasant view

Start by expecting the best intentions from others.
When they deliver it is joyful. When we expect to
be cheated or wronged, we suffer from anxiety and
anger while we await the outcome, whatever it
ends up being. If we are disappointed, there is no
harm as long as we are prepared.

July 19

• • •

Sherlock's stock in trade
Used on our self we learn much
Change is possible

Observation is a powerful tool. It increases our
awareness and brings to light useful facts. Used on
our self it means noticing what we do, or fail to do,
that gets in the way of reaching our goals. To build
our use of compassion we can notice what
behaviors we have that get in the way. We can
notice how often they happen, when they are most
likely to happen, who is around, where we are,
what we sense in our bodies, what conditions
preceded the behavior and so forth.

For example, I know I am prone to use harsh words
unnecessarily and that this is most likely to happen
with members of my immediate family when I am
stressed and feel I am being ignored or criticized. I
am aware that my lips get pursed and my breathing
is shallower when this is about to happen. By
knowing this, and paying attention to the clues, I
can avoid these actions more often and avoid
creating pain unnecessarily.

What can you learn about your own behaviors that
get in the way of compassion? Make notes every
time you notice yourself acting in a way that is

counter to your desire to be more compassionate. Do this every day for the next week. Then see how you can use what you observe to reduce how often those behaviors occur.

July 20

• • •

Taught since we were young
Strong values and good manners
Keep us from errors

Apologizing when wrong, making others whole
when your mistakes affect them, respecting others.
All those things we learned in kindergarten help
keep us out of harm's way or help ensure we
minimize the discomfort we might otherwise
cause. Knowing them is one thing, practicing them
faithfully and fully is another. What lesson learned
when you were young can you practice more
successfully?

Today is day 2 of the practice.

共感

July 21

• • •

Conscious attention
Our taking care of business
Makes the world go round

Keeping what's important front and center helps us
do what needs to be done to keep things on an
even keel. When that happens we create the
conditions that support wellbeing and reduce pain
and discomfort. Being clear with others about
what is most important helps create conditions
that allows them to respond in healthy and
productive ways. What can you do to be clearer
about what is most important, either for yourself
or what you expect or need from others? Spend
the next five minutes writing down ideas for doing
this and experiment with the ones that appeal to
you most.

Today is day 3 of the practice.

July 22

• • •

Mountain rises up
Majestic in its stature
Destiny calls us

When we are centered and grounded in who we are we are like a mountain, steadfast and quietly powerful. We are capable of being ourselves and living our lives as who we really are. Honoring yourself by letting your true self be seen is a good first step to reducing the suffering that results from not being who you are. This can be as simple as starting to voice your opinion when others might not agree, or wearing what your really want, or showing others the project you have secretly worked on. What is in your life that is being hidden? What can you start showing the world that lets more of you be seen?

Today is day 4 of the practice.

• • •

Clouds, winds, stars and moon
Close observation yields clues
Uncertainty melts

Understanding our environment is a necessary condition to effective action. Our ancestors studied the clues in the environment to determine weather patterns and planting cycles, allowing them to respond effectively to an uncertain world. The same is true when we want to grow our compassion. We can study our environment to know what actions are most supportive. For example, taking the time to understand someone's point of view, circumstances, or objective helps us respond more appropriately and helps us avoid making a situation worse by reacting poorly. Practice listening with a curious mind, one that seeks to understand what is behind someone's words or actions, before acting.

Today is day 5 of the practice.

• • •

Apart, then as one
Distant becomes intimate
Point of view changes

Taking a moment to really put ourselves in someone else's place changes our whole perspective of another. Try imagining your self physically and emotionally as the other person and sense how personal what they are saying or doing is to them. See how it affects your viewpoint or assumptions about them, their motives and motivations, and their humanity. Compassion will be much easier when you can see the world from the eyes of another.

Today is day 6 of the practice.

July 25

• • •

Lightning rips the sky
We jump and become alert
Potential released

Action creates change. What is compassion
without action? Keep track of how many times you
perform an act of compassion today.

Today is day 7 of the practice.

• • •

Slapped upside the head
Resentment smolders and burns
Cool waters save two

When someone betrays or intentionally hurts you the resentment is painful. Self-compassion provides multiple benefits in this situation. Certainly, recognizing your own pain and suffering, and alleviating it, improves your situation.   It also keeps you from adding to the original pain with self-imposed suffering that comes from returning to it again and again. Taking care of your self also creates the foundation for responding in a more considered way, and that is less likely to create further pain for all involved.

Start by acknowledging your own pain and state of being and then comparing it to how you would like to be.   With this perspective ask yourself what benefit there is to holding on to your anger, what is to be gained by staying in that place? What is given up by moving forward instead of stewing in the past? Let the inviting cool waters of where you want to be help you let go. Come back to that contrast again and again until you have let go of the pain and planted yourself firmly in a healthier place.

July 27

. . .

Child on bicycle
Peddling hard with wobbly wheels
Smiling, not frowning!

Out on a bike, putting their heart into riding, a child is hell-bent on pushing the boundaries and going forward. He or she is content that they doing their best to lean in to a challenge and making progress, even if the execution is far from perfect. That spirit points to the value of focusing on our intention vs. our results. Results are important. They give us feedback so that we can learn and improve if we wish. However, our intention is where we start. When we face a particularly tough challenge, and are critical of how we performed, we can practice self-compassion by considering the difference between our intention and our results. If our intention was honest and good we can dwell on that and let it continue to motivate us. If our results are less than perfect, we are learning, nothing more, nothing less. Remember the beauty of your intention and let it outshine your initial results.

• • •

Murky mists lay low
Ghosts and phantoms everywhere
Wait, nothing is there!

How easy is it to get trapped in a whole alternate reality when we are stressed? It can be easy to imagine every possible negative outcome and fall victim to scores of imagined malicious slights and setbacks. Before anything has even happened we are worked up and ready to attack. But if we pause and ask what is actually true, what is actually in front of us, we often find none of our imagined scenarios exists. Pause and reflect on what is known to be true and focus on that when stressed. Once you've broken the chain reaction, it makes sense to plan for contingencies but recognize them as no more than that.

• • •

Pebble into pond
Smiles reflecting quiet joy
A tender heart spreads

When we see the goodness around us we are
naturally lifted. That same experience is amplified
when those around us come in contact with that
spirit. Our joy fills us first and then others as our
joy spreads. Let your heart be tender and
appreciate the small things today: a cloud, the soft
colors of a field, your child's natural grace, the
pattern of birds flying overhead. Rest in that
experience and let it lift you and others.

• • •

Climbing the mountain
Brilliant views and painful tests
Our truth is revealed

Start practicing compassion with those who you don't like. Not just people who are in need but people who are actively annoying you. They may be people who carelessly bump into you, someone talking loudly in a movie, how about someone who just cut you off in traffic? You might find out just how many people you don't like! And you might also find a new perspective on your capacity to grow your compassion, and a rewarding view of what is possible.

July 31

• • •

Deflated balloon
Collapsed, sides stuck together
Waiting for fresh air

Everything comes apart now and then. When that
happens we can feel defeated, only able to feel and
see our own failures, with no energy to go forward.
Sometimes knowing that tomorrow is another day
and that you will try again is enough. Let whatever
is holding you down pass and then regroup when it
has.

August

August 1

• • •

Spilled milk on the floor
We want it to go away
What makes it so hard?

When we have hurt someone else we might
harden our heart and ignore what we have done.
But the pain inside doesn't go away. We have a
choice.   We can harden our hearts further by doing
nothing. Or we can make amends and admit we
were wrong. This can be hard when we fail to see
the pain we have caused the other person. Once
we own up to the hurt we have caused, and realize
we can help ease it, doing the right thing becomes
easier.

August 2

• • •

Smooth stone in river
Rolls along with the current
Gentle and polished

Sometimes the best way we can exercise
compassion for ourselves and for others is to go
along with the flow. How often do we really need
to disrupt things to get our way? Unless your
wellbeing is endangered, moving with and
supporting others provides delight for all involved.

August 3

• • •

Empty well, hot sun
With eyes closed we trudge onward
Cool nighttime awaits

When we are out of gas emotionally, physically, mentally, or spiritually, we often labor on. If we are compassionate we recognize at some point that we are only hurting ourselves by carrying on. We can always consider alternatives that offer better opportunities for accomplishing our goals. What decisions can you make to create or use the conditions that will allow this?

• • •

Mirror reflecting
Flawlessly revealing all
When is it enough?

If we are aware we can see patterns and habits
more clearly. If we practice this enough we cannot
ignore the places where we cause pain for others.
Maybe it is habitually ignoring someone, or
interrupting people mid-sentence, or letting your
frustration show at inappropriate times. Whatever
it is, practice noticing your impact on others and
then pick an area to intentionally change so that
you eliminate the distress you are adding to the
world.

• • •

Balcony is high
All around one sees action
The whole play and more

Have you ever stepped back and seen what is happening with a dispassionate view? We can practice this with our own thoughts and behaviors. Stepping out of the action to watch offers a more dispassionate perspective. Being practiced at having a bit of separation between ourselves and what is going on around us offers the ability to change events, much like in a play where we are the director. When we are able to do this intentionally we get to decide if we like what we are about to do, or agree to, or hold back from doing. We have opportunities to practice this on a regular basis. The next time you notice that you are uncomfortable on some level practice seeing the bigger picture and see what new possibilities you choose for how things unfold.

• • •

Anger boils over
Words like fists strike out to hit
What would momma say?

"When you've nothing good to say, don't say anything at all." These can be good words to live by when frustration brings us to the boiling point. Words can hurt just like fists. The difference is the damage can be hard to see. This alone can help us avoid making a bad situation worse. However, if all else fails, apply what you probably learned in kindergarten. A day later, if the issue still is present, address it while in a better state of mind. If the issue has become a distant memory, be thankful you were able to keep your mouth shut.

• • •

Cool river surrounds
Caressing with gentle touch
Can life be better?

Enjoy those moments when you are with loved ones and celebrating being together, even when it might be considered a splurge or being pampered. Those times are like sitting in a cool river on a warm summer day. The sun is on your face, the cool waters are gently rushing by you, and birds are chirping nearby. Yes, this will change and, yes, it comes at the expense of something else. But if a special moment is not to be enjoyed, when will we ever enjoy ourselves? Learning to appreciate the moment and being generous with others makes life richer and opens us to relaxing into what is available to us right now. Focus on the enjoyment and the connection and let anxieties and worries drop away. Find a time to bring pleasure to your friends or family by arranging to do something special with them.

August 8

• • •

**Prison walls surround
Two worlds, but no connection
The door can open**

When we are overly focused on defending our turf at every turn we can become walled off to what is happening all around us. In these conditions practicing and developing compassion is very difficult. When we are like this it often doesn't feel very good to us and it probably doesn't feel very good to others. The answer to changing this is clear; take time regularly throughout the day to tune into what is happening around you and adjust accordingly to create greater comfort for all involved.

August 9

• • •

Choppy seas at hand
Every throw yields empty nets
Put the nets away

Self-compassion benefits from wisdom.
Sometimes we keep trying to make a bad situation
better, thinking we are to blame or believing we
can make it better. There are times when this isn't
true. Knowing when that is is where wisdom
comes in. When we see that the conditions are
outside of our influence we can stop working so
hard to no avail. Ask yourself whether you own
any responsibility for the difficulty at hand or if you
truly have the means to make any difference. A
simple, "True, false, or I don't know" will suffice. If
"true," then work to make it right; if "false," then
stop and put your efforts where they will be more
useful; if "I don't know," then decide what you
need to learn to be able to get a clear answer.

August 10

• • •

**Odd shapes and colors
A scattered nonsense displayed
Prudence makes perfect**

A puzzle is many parts that are a scattered confusion when looked at collectively. When we examine where each might belong we find that harmony can be brought forth. So it is with these compassion practices. Selecting them for the right opportunity by applying different ones for different scenarios can help us bring order out of chaos. As you go about your day consider what practices you might use to the best effect.

August 11

• • •

Moms, Dads, spouses, kids
Tenderness runs throughout all
Compassion rises

See others as being like your own mom or dad or
any loved one who is dear to you. Know that they
are dear to someone in this same way and use that
tenderness to see him or her in a more
compassionate light.

• • •

Revolving door swings
Mad rush, we miss our exit
Ah, second chances!

Sometimes we are lucky enough to get a second chance. If you find an opportunity to make up for something you aren't feeling good about, take it! No need to wallow in past feelings. Forgive yourself if you are beating yourself up. Feelings come and go and you can take advantage of this by adjusting to a more appropriate outlook with the new opportunity. Going forward is more useful than revisiting the past.

August 13

• • •

Reflections of light
Dancing fantastically
Forever they change

When we realize our life is unfolding at every moment we can see that it is less solid and fixed than we may have thought. Understanding this makes it easier to let go of trying so hard to preserve something that is likely to change anyhow. Which in turn allows us to see new opportunities to evolve and change in ways that support wellbeing for others and ourselves. What better version of your self might exist in the next moment? What new choices can be made?

August 14

• • •

Rusty and dull blade
Made sharp again with great care
Others benefit

We are always affecting others. So when we take care of ourselves who benefits? When we are compassionate with ourselves and support ourselves we can do more.   What are some of the ways others benefit when you are able to say, "no" to what isn't healthy for you and instead take the time to do the things that make you stronger and more capable?   Take 10 minutes and make a list of how self-compassion can be good for you and for others.

August 15

• • •

Hazy bank of fog
Imagination runs wild
Truth waits to be found

How often do we judge someone or something based on a predisposition or story we have in our head? When we have few facts and just hazy images or perceptions it is easy to come to conclusions that harm others and us. Despite this, the truth can still be found for those who can shift from judging to learning. Notice whenever you are judging someone or something without the benefit of the facts. The more you notice this, the more you will be able to step back and find ways to fill in the blanks.

August 16

• • •

Hidden among us
We see but we don't observe
Nuggets everywhere!

Others have a lot to teach us about compassion.
Watch for it today, you are sure to see others
practicing it. What can you learn from them and
put into practice?

• • •

Unaware and dazed
New experiences unfold
We are more alive

Things sometimes happen when we least expect them. And, when they do, we often learn lessons that are lasting. Sometimes we try new things just so we can learn. Make today a day when you do this. Try writing your own compassion haiku about what you learn about compassion today.

August 18

• • •

**Star shining brightly
Restful, present, enchanting
Yet it "does" nothing**

Just letting ourselves "be" without thought or desire for an action or outcome is a rich self-compassion practice. Often, these are the times we most remember or treasure: sitting in a park, walking with a friend, resting in the shallow water of the sea. Take some time out to let the day or the moment develop as it will and simply appreciate it without working to make it anything other than what it is.

August 19

• • •

Tree laden with fruit
Available and wholesome
Why stay so hungry?

No matter who you are there are times you have been at your best. And in those times you did things that made you and the world a better place. Chances are some of those things are natural and appear in your life often. It may be ensuring that projects get finished, or helping soothe those who are upset, or solving difficult problems, or sharing stories that make people laugh or cry. It could be anything at all and if you take the time and allow yourself to see them you will. Whatever memories or traits you identify of you being the best version of you, take some to acknowledge what you do or have done well.

• • •

**A better planet
Isn't that what we all want?
Add, do not subtract**

Whether you are supporting yourself to be healthier and more content or doing the same for others, you are making the world a better place. Each of us has the means to help determine whether we experience life for better or for worse. Let that powerful realization be your motivation to keep compassion in the forefront of your mind as you move throughout your day.

August 21

• • •

Curiosity
Not good for longevity
If you are a cat

Of course, we are not cats. Instead, curiosity can be our friend. When we see something we don't understand, or don't like, curiosity can help us avoid distress. The next time you are annoyed or angry with another person, ask yourself what would explain the behavior or perspective that you are reacting to. When you know the whole story your reaction will most likely be far different and more compassionate.

• • •

Desert heat shimmers
Desperate travelers die
Dangerous mirage

When we live authentically we show ourselves as we really are. When we hide or change the view of who we are it is like a mirage, misleading others about what they will find when they interact with us. As a way of life it is hard to imagine how this benefits either those we engage with or us. What parts of your self do you hide or mask from the world? What can you change to be more authentic and avoid the inevitable pain that results from presenting your self as someone who you are not?

August 23

• • •

Horizon and sky
To be, each needs the other
Joined they are as one

Some things only exist because of another. Hot can be hot only when there is cold. How can cold exist if hot does not? When relationships like these exist one has to wonder if these things are ever really separated and independent. Where are the boundaries, what is between the end of one and the beginning of another? The same is true for you and me, or you and anyone else. It is by the existence of others that "me" acquires meaning. In a strange way that makes us dependent upon and extensions of each other. How would your behaviors and attitudes change if you saw everyone as an extension of yourself? If this is too much of a stretch consider how others are like you e.g. having a desire for friends, comfort, and health and deserve the same amount of care and consideration.

• • •

Rest and do nothing
Some recoil at such a thought
Unwittingly trapped

After work... rest. This is the time-honored pattern
our bodies and systems have lived by for millennia.
Nothing can go on forever. Eventually things break
when used too hard. Often we have a story that
we need to push though it and "stay productive."
Without realizing it we are setting ourselves up for
our own breakdown. Plenty of research shows that
resting on a regular cycle after exertion is the key
to optimal growth and functioning. Rest is
especially important when we are not well. Let
self-compassion win the day. Support your best
self with regular rest after exertion.

• • •

Mountains and molehills
Same shape yet not the same thing
Perspective matters

Small things can really be irritating and can prevent us from being our best. Viewed at ground level a molehill looks a lot like a mountain. Viewed from above we can see the vast difference between the two. Having a bigger perspective can often change how we see and react to situations and make them less troublesome. How can you invoke a bigger perspective in order to be more compassionate with yourself and others?

August 26

• • •

Joyful, glad feelings
Good will, glad tidings spread wide
Something from nothing

It is easy to see how a chain reaction of good will and joy can spread once it gets started. And that, of course, is the key. It must get started. And once it does, it is a whole lot easier to practice kindness and supporting others. Let taking the first step be your practice today. There is little to be lost in this and much to be gained.

August 27

• • •

Opportunity
Trying but not succeeding
It's the heart that counts

Sometimes we see an opportunity to help where
we can make a difference. And we do our best.
But it doesn't matter and the situation we hoped to
improve stays the same, or goes backwards. If our
intention and heart was true then we can let
ourselves off the hook. Make today's practice
about keeping your heart and intentions true in all
you do

August 28

• • •

Darkness foreboding
Evil in the shadows lurks
And is left waiting

What isn't done can also be an act of compassion.
Forgoing an impulse to do harm, especially when it
can be rationalized, is liberating. In that moment
you free yourself from evil's grip and your capacity
for compassion grows. Look for an impulse that
you can let go off as you go about your day.

• • •

Calm waters all around
A quiet day of smooth sailing
Captain is challenged

Sometimes I find that minding my own business is
the most compassionate thing I can do. I stay out
of trouble and others are not bothered. Perhaps
you have had the same experience. However,
there is a line between being too engaged and not
engaged enough. What can you learn about when
keeping to yourself is the best policy?

August 30

• • •

Teeter-totter sits
One end up, the other down
Each needs the other

Being able to fully exercise and develop our compassion requires a certain sense of equality and balance. To be able to give it without judgment we must be able to accept it without reservation. To love others we must be able to love ourselves. We need boundaries that keep our relationships from getting lopsided. How can you use these ideas to strengthen your ability to offer genuine compassion?

• • •

Floating on the top
What could be more natural?
No longer held down

When we stop getting down on ourselves we naturally rise up, like a buoy in the water.   And we will stay there unless we put ourselves down again. If you have a long time habit of perfectionism or self-criticism or feeling inadequate, rising up and feeling buoyant may not feel natural. Use that image to give yourself the luxury of that experience, and holding on to it, until it becomes natural. Appreciate that you are here and take pleasure in being able to make choices that are helpful.

共感

September

September 1

• • •

Winter's deep slumber
Stark but so necessary
Spring needs winter

Without a winter spring cannot occur. Winter's rest provides the conditions needed for new growth. Some things in life cannot be shortcut. Recognize this and alternate effort with rest in order to nurture yourself and others.

• • •

We scratch our itches
Not exactly a surprise
Yet remarkable

Without even thinking about it we often instinctively relieve minor annoyances effortlessly. Compassion can be like this. Often it happens without our even noticing. Just as scratching an itch can be unconscious so can our acts of compassion. Notice today how often you act, or intentionally don't act, in order to ease the way for yourself or for others. Keep a log and make note of them. You may be surprised at how instinctive those acts are and how often they occur. Regardless, see what you can learn about your compassion habits and what makes them easy and natural.

September 3

· · ·

A key and a lock
Sweet harmony in action
Soft click reassures

Our enjoyment and capacity for compassion is
heightened when we are leveraging our natural
strengths. This is true in any realm; we get the
greatest enjoyment when we are using what is
natural for us. How much easier is it to do work
that calls on your best attributes than doing work
where you have limited skill? Take an inventory of
what your do best. Now, use that knowledge to be
more intentional about where you might exercise
compassion.

• • •

Deep wish sounds within
Before all else, do no harm
Relief and freedom

Knowing that we have at times intentionally been the source of others' pain is a heavy weight that we must fully sense and absorb. Our acceptance of this knowledge leads us to the deeply grounded wish that we do no harm. Working towards that end brings relief and freedom from continuing to live in the ignorance that harms others and us. Put yourself in the shoes of someone who you intentionally hurt and feel the pain they experienced. Now recognize how it was caused by you. Let the result you created sink in as a truth and vow to never intentionally be the source of pain again.

• • •

Safety net strung tight
Prep is done, lessons are taught
Time now to let go

Getting out of the way allows growth to be tested and refined. It's likely you can see how this applies to others, e.g. letting children take on new responsibilities, asking a new team member to take on something new after they've been shown the basics, not being available to do something for a friend after showing her how to do it on her own. However, how does this apply to you? Where are those places where you shrink back from trying on new behaviors that will make you stronger, even when you have the basic skills and the risk is not life or death? What could be more self-compassionate than giving yourself the opportunity to develop new ways to thrive? Where can you let go of overly protecting yourself in ways that limit you?

• • •

"Why do you rob banks?"
"'Cause that's where the money is"
Some things are simple…

Urban legend has it that the notorious bank robber, Willie Sutton, famously explained his habit of robbing banks in the simple exchange quoted above. The simplicity of the answer overwhelms any further discussion. What Willie Sutton made obvious was that if we want to achieve something we go where the opportunity is. And so it is with practicing compassion. If we want to increase our practice and expand our capacity, we should increase our awareness of opportunities that present themselves. For example, instead of walking by someone who looks like someone they need help, we should stop and ask if we can help. Simple, right? See what opportunities you can act on today.

• • •

Balloon inflating
Boundaries stretch easily
Pop! Balloon no more

We enjoy seeing that balloon get bigger with each breath. Then, suddenly, pop! It is no more. We are like that balloon. When we stretch our boundaries too far, our own lives break down. Being compassionate can be seductive leading us to continually make more room for others. But it can be taken to an extreme, leading to a breakdown in our health and quality of life. If we want to increase our capacity for compassion we must also tend to our own needs.   Failure to do so will only limit our own ability to grow and contribute. Eventually failure to care for ourselves becomes counter-productive and more harm than good is created.

What needs of yours must continually be protected in order for your wellbeing to remain intact? How diligently are you protecting them? What can you do ensure they are protected?

September 8

• • •

Pacing… more pacing…
Running free, now soaring high
Feet leaving the ground

Sometimes we limit our compassion to things we can "solve" or "fix" in order to reduce our own or other's suffering. Providing more opportunity, embracing more possibility is another form of practicing compassion that we might overlook. How are your beliefs and actions keeping yourself or others penned in? What might you change in order to open up new horizons?

September 9

• • •

Fire, ready, aim, whoops!
Splat, splat, splat, targets explode
Stomach sinks, now what?

How often has this happened to you? After
reacting in anger some part of you knows that your
attack was a mistake. What happens then? Do you
rationalize what has happened and let the storm
run its course? Do you back off and hope for the
best? Do you seek to understand what happened
and make amends? Some of these choices create
more pain for others and for us. Remember that it
is never too late for compassion.

September 10

• • •

Weak and out of breath
Desire pushes us further
Gain turns into loss

Even when our intention is good we can do harm
by taking actions that are beyond our capacity.
Knowing our practical limits (whether they be
physical, intellectual, emotional, financial, etc.),
and what we are getting involved with, are good
guardrails for helpful compassion.

• • •

Evil eye at work
In anger we wish the worst
Darkness blankets all

How often does the irritation of someone's actions lead us down the path of wishing something bad on someone, even if it is relatively mild like, "I hope this happens to them someday!" I'm guessing we all can admit to having secretly wished ill will on someone. Yet, wouldn't it be more effective if that person were to suddenly become more understanding or loving or compassionate? How can it help anyone, including us, if they suffer? The next time you find yourself getting annoyed or angered by someone else try wishing them well, seeing them with the positive traits that would make them a valued friend.

• • •

Dark and soundless room
Trepidation threatens us
Trust in self trumps all

Sometimes we face situations that we are
unfamiliar with. If the stakes are high enough we
can find ourselves focusing on how we might fail.
Before you know it, we've got butterflies in the
stomach and we can name all sorts of disasters
that await us. But when we look into our
storehouse of experience and skills and
accomplishments, and accept our strengths, we
find we can manage just fine. Imagine all that you
have ever done, every challenge you have ever
met, every failure you've bounced back from, every
mistake you have learned from, every triumph you
have had, and all of your years of deep experience
as a thick, giant tail firmly supporting you. Develop
a deep sense of trust from resting in the comfort of
that storehouse of wisdom that is yours.

September 13

· · ·

Glittering like gold
False hope carries destruction
Shame and tragedy

When we have the privilege of being trusted we
have the duty to protect. When we are in a
position where we have the advantage, it can be
tempting to paint a better picture than what is,
especially if it benefits us. Overcoming that
temptation is compassion practiced twice. We put
others in a position to make better choices and we
avoid damaging our own integrity and character.
Hold yourself to the highest standard when
interacting with others and treat their interests as
they would want them treated.

共感

September 14

• • •

Bright light fills the room
The world becomes inviting
It's just that simple

Research shows that positive emotions lead us to become more creative, improve our health, increase our curiosity and interest in the world, boost our optimism, and have better social relationships.   Simply appreciating the good things in life can be one of the best things you do for yourself. Spend a little extra time savoring those moments.

• • •

Common courtesy
Sun shines, waters calm, breeze cools
Why be so stingy?

Compassion can be spontaneous. We might automatically help someone with a package, or smile at a stranger, or let someone know we appreciate what he or she does. Simply saying, "please" makes things more pleasant. All of those things, often referred to as, "common courtesy," have an impact and they are both easy and free! Knowing this, you can increase your compassion instantly by simply practicing them more often. Why be stingy, indeed?

September 16

• • •

Slumped and exhausted
Gasping for breath we breathe deep
Stronger we become

When we push ourselves beyond our normal limits, and then recover, we become stronger and more capable. So it is with compassion. Consider that next time you are being tried. Recognize it as an opportunity to grow your capacity.

September 17

• • •

Deep drop just ahead
Ground disappears and time stops
Look before you leap!

Not everyone wants to be helped. When we cross
that line we know it. If we are observant, we can
see it as we approach. Learn and pay attention to
the signs that tell you when you are too close. Be
good to yourself and to others and respect those
boundaries when you come across them.

September 18

• • •

Masquerade party
Do we see that masks are worn?
Or just fantasy

Every day we deal with people who show us only a small part of who they really are. What we see is likely to be just a surface reality. When we recognize that we can then remind ourselves that there are many facets to their being that we do not know. Before we settle on a judgment it is good to consider other explanations that might exist.
Doing so will open us up to a more compassionate stance.

• • •

Constant companion
Always ready to support
Oddly forgotten

We really are our own best friends, when we choose to be. No one is with us more often or can support us so readily. So why not make use of this as regularly as needed or desired? Start your day with a silent reminder that you have, can, and will successfully navigate the day-to-day challenges of life. When challenged remind yourself that you will be there for yourself; recall the good decisions you've made and recognize that you will make more of them. All of these things and more are available to you every day at any time. Make use of them.

September 20

• • •

Dominos standing
Delicate balance at play
Which way will it be?

When we make a mistake we have some choices
ahead of us. We can ignore or deny them or we
can own up to them. When we ignore them we set
off a chain reaction and one misfortune leads to
another as our mistakes compound.   When we
acknowledge them, and work to make it right, we
can short-circuit that chain reaction. Doing so
saves others and ourselves untold pain. It's the
compassionate thing to do.

• • •

Calm sea all around
How long can we enjoy it?
Waves are far away

One way to handle challenging situations is to start with a peaceful mind. Like the sea, with enough agitation we will eventually become disturbed. But it takes a lot more to turn a calm sea into rough waters than it does to turn a light chop into a dangerous place to be. So what is the lesson here? Having a settled mind gives you a strong foundation to move through difficult times more effectively. When you are calm and composed you, and everyone else you are dealing with, benefit. A regular meditation practice is one way to do this.

共感

September 22

• • •

Clear blue morning sky
Bright sun passes overhead
Nighttime once again

Today is the autumnal equinox (at least in the northern hemisphere), when day and night are closest to being of equal length during the year. Let this natural cycle be a metaphor for even-handedness and equanimity. Being able to experience life's ups and downs with equal acceptance serves as a foundation for your compassion. Be kind to yourself and make equanimity your practice today. Recognize that what is true today will be different tomorrow and temper your response accordingly.

• • •

Compass and needle
Pointing north we navigate
Need somewhere to go

Compassion grows from thoughtful choices. Knowing what results we want helps us choose actions that create the right conditions. What is it you want to nurture for yourself? What is the better version of you that you wish to develop? Consider this carefully so that you can choose those things that will support you on your journey.

• • •

**Stately pyramid
Cannot be easily moved
Here for the ages**

We can take a lesson from the great pyramids of Egypt. Without their massive base and foundation they could not rise so high and last so long. So it is with our capacity for compassion. The stronger we make our foundation, the more we can offer to others. Without it, we become unsteady and unable to support much. We can think of our base in terms of multiple dimensions, e.g. physical, emotional, mental, and spiritual. Where are you strong? What needs to be stronger? What is a step you can take today to begin the process of strengthening your ability to offer more to the world?

September 25

• • •

Ice sliding on ice
Neither resists the other
All becomes easy

When we have no expectations of receiving
anything in return for our compassion, and we are
in tune with the needs of others, there is no
friction to impede our efforts. Practice giving
where your sole focus is to help reduce the distress
of others. Notice what works and what doesn't in
those efforts.

September 26

• • •

Big and empty hole
Looms larger for what it lacks
One act changes all

There can be times when we see that we've left
important things unattended, like exercising
compassion (!). No need for regret or denial,
simply look around and act where the opportunity
presents itself.

September 27

• • •

Humming deep inside
Anticipation spills forth
Meets ice cold water

Sometimes we want something so bad that when
we offer it to someone else we get a rude
awakening and find they aren't as interested as we
are! Maybe we didn't really want to help them as
much as we wanted to satisfy our own desires. Has
this ever happened to you? How can you recognize
when you are setting yourself up for this? Pay
attention to when your excitement about
something is greater than the other party's. When
that happens, stop and recognize that what you are
planning on offering may not be compassion at all.
Focus on your connection to others and on seeing
what is important to them.

September 28

• • •

Opportunity
Target rich environment
Pick some for practice

Whatever it is we want to improve, intentional practice has a way of increasing our skill and capacity. Of course, we all know this. Everywhere we go there are opportunities to practice connecting with others and helping support their wellbeing. Just pick one and practice. Consider being intentional about what skill or skills to practice as well. Not sure where to begin? Listening, sensing what it is like to be in their shoes, or being thoughtful about how to best support them are some basics to start with.

共感

September 29

• • •

A left and a right
Choices are always present
Both are very real

Sometimes we get stuck on a habit or way of
thinking. Sooner or later we identify with it and
becomes part of who we are. In fact, we find
ourselves identifying with it. It becomes like a
familiar signpost that lets us know we are on
comfortable ground. But the amazing thing is that
we can, if we wish to, see the same situation in
multiple other ways. We always have other
choices we can make. While unfamiliar, a new way
is no less real than the one we have come to accept
as who we are. Do we suddenly go away when our
familiar ways no longer exist? Is it worth giving up
who you are today in order to be more satisfied
and capable? What counter-productive ways of
thinking or acting have become ingrained into your
self-image? What will it take to recognize them as
having as much substance as a phantom? What
new ways of being will you choose to try out
instead? Try one out today.

September 30

• • •

Glorious vista
Burning lungs and exhaustion
Which do you think of?

Motivation is often a matter of focusing on the rewards instead of the effort. So it is with compassion.

October

October 1

• • •

Open space freed up
Life and action on display
New truths are revealed

Sometimes the best way to support others is to get
out of the way. When we exit the stage or take a
back seat we make room for others to learn, grow,
and enjoy their own moment. Are there places in
your life where you are taking up too much space?

October 2

• • •

**Love your enemy
Disconcerting isn't it?
What if they were helped?**

Compassion that only includes our loved ones and
friends is incomplete. If we want to grow our
capacity for compassion we must offer it to
everyone. This can be challenging. After all,
enemies have done us wrong, they mean to harm
us. But what if they were more loving, more
compassionate, more joyful, and more level-
headed themselves? What if we helped them
reach that state? Wouldn't we be better off for it?
Practice seeing your enemy filled with love, with
compassion, with joy, and with equanimity. When
that becomes easier, start acting from that
perspective.

• • •

Meek, mild, and weakened
Positivity matters
Down but never out!

That's the beauty of compassion. No matter what your position is in life, you can always make a contribution to the wellbeing of all. A great deal of research shows that a positive mood brings multiple benefits. And, have you ever noticed how simply being around someone who is positive brightens your own mood? Knowing that we can brighten lives (including our own) by being positive gives us something to feel positive about! No matter what circumstances you face today, recall that you can practice compassion simply by doing something to lift your own and others' moods.

共感

October 4

• • •

**Beautiful vista
Invites us to calmly rest
No need to achieve**

Even compassion can be a trap. If we are doing it
out a sense of duty or obligation or achievement
we have to ask what is being served. We can relax
and let it arise on its own when the time is right.
Notice if you are "checking a box" and, if you are,
let yourself off the hook. Stop and smell the roses.

• • •

Far out on a limb
Slow… slow… drooping… creaking sounds
Crash!! … or crawl back in?

Knowing our limits is important in compassion.
Sometimes we find out by going to far. Sometimes
we notice the signals. What signals get your
attention? Pay attention to what you sense when
you creep out on a limb.

• • •

A web with no strings
Morning dew shows up elsewhere
Source of beauty lost

Without connection compassion cannot be practiced. So, a first step towards practicing compassion is to connect with others. Sometimes that means making ourselves vulnerable and providing an opening for others to connect with us. Sometimes it is making the first move to reach out and engage truthfully and in earnest with someone else. Sometimes it means being open to the possibility that others have a valid opinion. Sometimes it is something else. What are some ways you can create more connections with others?

October 7

• • •

Hibernating bears
Winter's ruin avoided
Live another day

Taking care of ourselves when under serious stress is essential, even though we may not be of much benefit to others during these times. We ensure our ability to contribute to the wellbeing of all by taking care of ourselves first during these times. Let yourself off of the hook when you need to scale back.

• • •

Key in your pocket
Fits the lock to free their pain
Now we must decide

This often describes our situation. We have
something that will relieve the suffering of another.
What will it take to use it? What keeps us from
doing so? Compassion is easier and more natural
when we have dealt with these questions and
resolved our uncertainty. Warning: These
questions may seem easier on paper than in real
life!

October 9

• • •

Wisdom exercised
No doubts, the right thing is done
Trouble is avoided

Wisdom is a great aid to practicing compassion. When we have experienced enough, and have paid attention to the lessons, we find it easier to avoid confrontation. There are times when stepping back from potential danger is the best option, the only option, for avoiding danger. Let your wisdom overcome your ego and avoid creating more suffering. Learn to pay attention to what you know to be right.

October 10

• • •

Leaves glide in the air
Reaching the ground they now rest
What more is needed?

This is to celebrate and recognize those days where we have been supportive of ourselves, kind to others, and have nothing we are striving for. Embrace these days and moments just as they are. There is nothing else to do.

• • •

Selfless sacrifice
All thoughts and deeds for others
One big family

Parents often put their children ahead of themselves. Everything they do for their children is intended to reduce the suffering they will face in the world. When that unconditional love is extended to all, our world will be forever changed. What will it take to see everyone the way you would see a daughter, or a son, or a mom or dad or other cherished loved ones? Picture them in that relationship to you and let the connection begin to grow.

October 12

• • •

Friend in need calling
Tested by our second thoughts
We learn what's inside

There are times when we feel tested when others
call on us for support. Those are the times we
learn where our boundaries are. How much can
we give and still honor what we need for
ourselves? A chance for us to grow and a chance
for us to give all rolled into one. Keep this in mind
the next time you are challenged this way.

• • •

Long and dusty road
Weary and tired we trudge home
Straight to bed we go!

When we are beat from a difficult day it is more
important than ever to be good to ourselves.
Despite the temptation to complete one more task,
it is time to exercise self-compassion and retire
from the day without guilt. Rested, we will be in a
better position to connect with others in a loving
way.

October 14

• • •

Unsteady toddler
Falls, walks, wobbles, falls again
Keeps moving forward

Compassion can be hard to practice. Sometimes
we aren't very aware or in control and find
ourselves acting in less than compassionate ways.
We can use these experiences to learn. Where did
we lose sight of our compassion, what hooked us,
how could we have responded differently? The
important thing is that we keep doing our best.

October 15

• • •

One shining moment
Radiant and glorious
The world melts away

When we genuinely connect with others it can be overwhelming in its impact. For the briefest of moments we are joined. And in that moment, all of life's familiar landmarks and challenges seem to melt away. Experiencing this requires vulnerability on our part as we let go of our separateness. Focus on the beauty in these moments as motivation for bringing more of it into being.

October 16

• • •

**Autumn tree stands still
Leaves drop and branches are bare
Makes way for new growth**

Letting go of old habits that no longer serve us can be hard. We momentarily lose our identity when we give them up. Who are we without them? That person hasn't been invented yet and for a time we stand barren, like the winter tree. And, like the tree, it is a necessary step to allow new growth and a dramatic change. Part of self-compassion is exercising the courage to step out of old ways that provide the comfort of familiar ground. What would you like to let go of that no longer serves you? Take a moment to write it down.

Now, what can you do to make that a reality? Perhaps sharing your plan with a friend, or sending reminder emails to yourself, or rewarding yourself for each sign of progress will help bring the plan into action. Take a moment to write down whatever ideas work for you.

October 17

• • •

Anger heating up
Whistle blows and we take heed
We can try again

One of the most helpful skills we can build for increasing our compassion is awareness. When we notice our heart is hard we can soften it. Knowing the signals that our walls are up is the key. When you are angry or closed off, pay attention to what you notice. Maybe your breath is shallower or more rapid, or maybe your lips are pursed, or your chest is tight. Whatever the clues, note them and become familiar with them. Use that knowledge to give yourself the chance to adjust.

October 18

• • •

**Fog, clouds, mist, and haze
Dangerous navigation
Let the sun shine bright!**

When we hide or shade what we believe or think, we make it hard for others to know what we mean. As a result, mistakes get made, relationships are damaged, and constructive dialogue doesn't happen. Transparency and clarity are the cure. Practicing them is exercising compassion by minimizing unintended suffering and problems.

October 19

• • •

Heart exposed to all
Risks taken and presence felt
Deeper connection

Being connected in a sense that we feel lifts others
and increases our attunement with others. This is
fertile ground for growing our compassion. It can
be practiced in simple ways. Try looking at every
person you come in contact with today. Not just
glancing at them, actually looking in their eyes and
acknowledging them as you pass by or talk with
them. Doing this, you also let yourself be seen and
take down some of the walls that separate us.

October 20

• • •

Scattered on the ground
Trees drop once beautiful leaves
Bigger things to come

Supporting ourselves to be healthier and more
satisfied is the essence of self-compassion. Letting
go of that which we've held on to, but no longer
serves us, gives us room to grow and thrive.
Review your relationships, your activities, thoughts,
and your habits. What ones are no longer serving
you? What roads are you not taking because of the
energy or time they take up?

What support can you create for yourself to
practice letting go of these in the days, weeks, and
months ahead? Write down whose help you can
enlist, tools or resources you can use, or changes
you can make to make this possible.

• • •

Painful agonies
Shrink in the face of the truth
Don't borrow trouble

It is easy to run away with our emotions. We feel so much larger and important when we get caught up in them. We seethe and agonize about the injustice or the crushing blows of whatever we are experiencing. The torment grows the more we linger in it. But if we step back and test how much of what we are feeling is actually true we see that we are often only borrowing trouble that doesn't exist. Of all the troubles you imagine when caught up in your emotions, test what is actually true right then, in that moment.

共感

October 22

• • •

Direction made clear
Guiding self on the journey
We choose our best route

Knowing our purpose is like knowing where we are headed. Without purpose we can only hope that fate is kind. With purpose we can make choices that suit our journey and experience greater joy and satisfaction. Finding our purpose takes reflection and objectively seeing where we are most engaged and alive. Denying our purpose is a recipe for living a less satisfying life. Do whatever it takes to attend to this critical self-need. Read books on this topic, journal, get coaching, and or attend a workshop designed for this purpose to help clarify yours.

• • •

Easy to confuse...
Duty versus compassion
Both get the job done

Motivation matters. Compassion does not spring from a desire to fulfill an obligation. Compassion comes from an open heart that reaches out to help others. Which motivates your actions when you help others? Both duty and compassion are noble and have a positive effect. One, however, is likely to go deeper than the other. When our hearts are open we have a deeper understanding of others. We are better equipped to offer help that is felt on more than one level.   Think about the compassion that you offer to others. Is it coming from a sense of duty or an open heart? If you sense that duty is playing too big a role, open your heart and allow yourself to feel what others are experiencing.

October 24

• • •

Pyramids rise high
One layer upon the next
Ground layer rocks!

If we take care of ourselves we can take care of others. Without a strong base there is only so much we can support. Caring for ourselves benefits more than just us. What does it take for you to be strong enough to lend your support to others? Whether it is sleep, exercise, play, time with loved ones, attending to your faith, honoring your values, savoring your strengths and your accomplishments, grieving, forgiving yourself, or anything at all that takes care of you, recognize how important it is and do it.

October 25

• • •

Deep love rests within
Hidden by the ugliness
Put on new glasses

We can always see the beauty within others if we try. Inside every woman is a loving mother. Inside every man is a loving father. Can it be hidden by ugly actions and mean words? Yes, of course. Can it be hidden by our own hardness? Absolutely. We can't control what others do or say, but we can control how we see them. Choose to see the good that is within them.

• • •

Open hearts expand
We all reach for love, not hate
Imagine that world

When we tap into the well of love we hold inside
we can give it away freely. When we think about a
world where everyone lives from that same place
we can imagine a heaven on earth. What is
stopping such a world from existing? Nothing is,
other than the participation of each of us. By
exercising compassion freely you are removing one
barrier to that world and inviting others to do the
same. Contemplate that today.

October 27

• • •

Deep, bottomless well
Try giving away your love
Pail is always full

When we practice compassion we find that as we give it out more wells up to take its place. Building your capacity for compassion happens whenever you practice it. Greet as many challenges as you find with compassion and keep at it all day. Notice how true compassion is always within us.

October 28

• • •

Up, down, up, down, up…
Rising becomes a habit
What other choices?

Not all of our efforts to be open, genuine, vulnerable, and caring are successful. What is important is that we continue to try again and again without giving up. As sure as the tides we return again and again. Unlike the tides we find that, with continued practice, we are able to stay a little longer

• • •

**No invitations
What compassion can we show?
Harmony is good**

Sometimes opportunities to be compassionate don't show themselves. And then we realize compassion is not just about relieving suffering. Practicing compassion isn't always something calling to us. It can also be about not creating any suffering in the first place. Recognizing the good in others and staying in harmony with that helps us avoid difficult situations that create discomfort or pain. Practice seeing the good in others. Respect and support that.

• • •

Shade tree grows taller
Provides shelter and relief
True for us as well

A tree, properly nourished and cared for, provides homes for birds, shade for people, and cover for animals. The same is true for us. When we take care of ourselves others benefit. By learning to take care of our needs, we are able to serve others more effectively, we are able to teach others how to care for themselves, and are able to empathize more effectively with their challenges. What challenges are you facing? What help can you seek to overcome these and, in so doing, put yourself in a position to pass that wisdom on to others?

共感

October 31

•   •   •

Stranger stands nearby
We see more than a person
Kindred spirits all

When we realize that others are fathers and
mothers, sisters and brothers, loved ones and
friends, we can see them as kindred spirits. We see
they could be our father or mother or brother or
sister or lover or friend. We can open our heart
more easily when we see our common humanity.

November

• • •

**Buried deep inside
Horrors waiting to be found
If only we knew**

"If we could read the secret history of our enemies, we should find in each man's life sorrow and suffering enough to disarm all hostility." Henry Wadsworth Longfellow wrote these words over 150 years ago. I wrote about these earlier but they bear repeating. They offer sound advice on what to contemplate when faced with attacks from our enemies or those who dislike or mistreat us. What could this person have faced in their past that would explain who they are. What sorrow and suffering have they faced? With this attitude we can take a more compassionate approach to the challenge they offer.

November 2

• • •

Bottom of the well
Lonely and trapped, what to do?
Don't go it alone!

How low do we have to go before we are willing to
seek support or help from others? What keeps us
from reaching out in order to take care of
ourselves? Brené Brown in *The Gifts of
Imperfection* points out that when we attach
judgment to receiving help we are also attaching
judgment to giving help. In other words, if we are
to give with an open heart we must be capable of
receiving with an open heart. A powerful way to
practice this is to make ourselves vulnerable by
exposing our imperfections and asking for help
from those who can provide it. (No one ever said
this was easy!) What help have you held off asking
for? Use one of those opportunities to practice
receiving in a non-judgmental and accepting way.

November 3

• • •

Dark clouds overhead
Raindrops fall down on our heads
Offering a choice

Have you ever been on a walk and found yourself underneath a steady rain, with no shelter nearby? You can either welcome the rain or let it ruin your walk. How we respond to challenging situations tells us a lot about ourselves. As it relates to compassion, everyday situations do the same thing. They remind us (all the time!) of how we interpret and respond to our world. Pay attention to these everyday situations and how you respond, they are our best teachers. They provide clear feedback on our development opportunities.

November 4

• • •

Nothing is sacred
Easy to say, hard to do
New heights await us

Learning the art of letting go is invaluable. When
we are willing to let go of our ingrained ways of
perceiving, our snap judgments and assumptions
give way to deeper and more nuanced
understanding. When we hold less tightly to ideas
we can become more open to new ideas and less
defensive. Through letting go of our stories we can
see the truth of others more clearly. All of these
help us develop compassion.   Make room for other
perspectives by reminding yourself of the value of
letting them in.

共感

• • •

Massive cliffs, sky high
From on high we feel mighty
No one can reach us

Our anger is like those massive cliffs. When we are in full blow fury we feel powerful and mighty. And, no one can reach us. Our hearts and our minds are closed.   Others cannot connect with us and we cannot connect with others. There is no room for compassion. We've all heard about counting to ten when we are angry. It is a good practice to use. It allows us to calm down enough to ask ourselves if being closed off and suffering from damaged relationships is really what we want for ourselves.

November 6

• • •

**Large oak by the stream
Silent yet present it soothes
A refuge for all**

We can offer compassion in the simplest of ways.
Among these is being there when others need a
steady presence. Deeply listening without
judgment is a rare gift. It gives others a place to
cool their emotions, allows them to be felt when it
is most helpful, and helps them sort out what is
important.

• • •

Unobstructed view
In plain sight we show ourselves
Courage born of trust

When we trust ourselves enough to be genuine we are more able to connect in a meaningful way with others. By being vulnerable we open up new avenues for reaching others. We are able engage in honest dialogue and spend less energy worrying about our positioning and more energy on what is actually helpful. Practice saying exactly what is in your heart and mind and being clear with yourself and others about how you feel.

November 8

. . .

Sun is overhead
Half of the day is now gone
Ready to start work

Sometimes we don't realize what is happening until we are in the middle of it. That means it isn't too late to affect the outcome. When we see ourselves acting in ways that will only cause pain and suffering (like in the middle of a heated argument) it is a chance to change course. It doesn't matter that we've misspent prior opportunities and veered off-course. What matters is we've been given an opportunity to get it back on track. Hallelujah! Pay attention to those early warning signs that clue you in to your harmful behavior. It may be your posture, it may be your tone of voice, your breathing, the way you wave your arms, your heart pounding, or any number of tells. Get to know them intimately. Then you can see what is happening before it is too late.

November 9

• • •

Big smiles and bright eyes
Come from play, not by design
Funny how that works!

Play is natural and happens without any concern for future payoffs. In fact, can you imagine it any other way? Can you imagine thinking about whether or not you are having enough fun when horsing around with your kids or joking with your friends? In fact, if we entered into play with expectations of certain outcomes, it's likely that it would no longer be play. Compassion works this way as well. If we enter into it with expectations of specific outcomes it loses its essence. Strengthen your compassion by giving up any expectations of a payoff.

November 10

• • •

Shoes worn by others
New perspective when put on
How to walk in them?

It's hard to offer help to others when we do not understand their experience. Before we walk in another's shoes, we first have to take off our own. Dropping our own perspective long enough in order to receive another's is a capability we can develop. Like all things, it requires practiced awareness and conscious choice. What tells you when you are holding tightly to your own perspective? How can you increase your awareness of this so that you can open up some space to truly understand another's?

共感

November 11

• • •

High bar or low bar?
Step or jump, which will it be?
Why is there a bar?

When we measure everything we do we can never be satisfied. We will always be focused on something we don't have or holding on to something we did. Practice having no bar. When you find yourself motivated to do or be something solely for the purpose of meeting or holding on to a measure, it is time to let go of it. Then you will be free to do what serves you.

November 12

• • •

Wooden water wheel
Effortlessly it turns round
Just needs the water

By practicing compassion every day we build up a
certain momentum where it becomes natural and
easy. If you've been sticking with the daily
practices you already know this. One of the best
ways to expand our capacity for compassion is to
continue to practice it every day. Let the peaceful
image of the waterwheel encourage you to keep it
turning.

November 13

• • •

Pit in the stomach
Impossible to ponder
Let that remind you

When we get angry and lash out or hurt someone
intentionally we feel it. We know we've done
something that may not be reversible. We can try
to make it right. But we should not forget how it
makes us feel when we've hurt someone and
realize what we've done. We should hold onto
that sick feeling as a reminder of what exists in all
of us. Let it serve as a reason to dedicate ourselves
to being compassionate.

November 14

• • •

Shifting forms ahead
Fear runs deep and vision blurs
Until we connect

Our storylines about others run deep. They color
our perceptions and often fly under the radar.
They can keep us living in separate worlds.
Compassion cannot thrive in these conditions.
These are barriers we put up ourselves. We are
responsible for them. We can drop them or
override them. Either way, we cannot know others
for who they are until we actually connect. Only
then can compassion be expressed. Identify the
stories you have about others. Challenge them so
that those barriers become weaker.

共感

• • •

Shields up, weapons armed
What is being protected?
What is to be gained?

When we get angry we puff ourselves up and defend our sense of importance. But when we are angry our shields go up and compassion is lost. Is the trade-off worth it? What, exactly, are we protecting? What do we have to gain? Are our opinions so valuable and fragile that we have to protect them? Are we so uncertain about ourselves that we have to harden our sense of self? To be clear, we need to defend ourselves from abuse that is harmful to us. However, how often do we even remember what it was that triggered our anger yesterday or the day before? The next time you feel that flash of anger, ask yourself what it is that is being protected; what is to be gained by shutting down? Is either worth the cost?

November 16

• • •

Car on the roadside
No one put in any gas
Passengers now walk

The reverse of this is true as well. When we take
care of business things run more smoothly. Here's
a reminder to take the time to make sure your
needs are being taken care off. Simple things like
sleep, healthy food, bills paid on time, exercise,
and sharpening your skills keep your life on track.
Learning to care for ourselves allows us to care for
others.

November 17

• • •

Smooth rock beneath us
We are steadied, soothed, and calmed
There when we need it

Inside each of us is the capacity to care for
ourselves when challenged. When we befriend
ourselves with a conscious commitment to be on
our own side we regain our confidence. We
literally become self-assured. Remind yourself of
this by saying to yourself, "I will stay right here with
you" the next time you feel cornered or unsure of
yourself.

November 18

· · ·

Water in a stream
At home, natural, and free
How else could it be?

Water has no contrivances when flowing in a
stream. Let it be a model for your compassion. It
is natural, unbridled, with no agenda other than to
flow where it is can be received. Let your
compassion be instinctive, without a hidden
agenda, and freely given where it can help. If you
find yourself forcing it or having an agenda other
than helping another, then step back and consider
what is actually taking place.

November 19

• • •

View from the hillside
We see the past behind us
How far we have come!

Every so often it pays to look back at what we have
faced and what we have managed to accomplish or
overcome. Perhaps reading an old journal, or
reminiscing over old pictures. Maybe just visiting
with old friends. We are reminded that we are still
here after facing many difficult challenges. While
we can't see ahead of us we can take comfort in
knowing we have shown ourselves to be capable of
navigating what life has put before us. Take
comfort in the distance you have traveled and
appreciate the strength you have inside.

共感

November 20

• • •

Small room we live in
Treasures gathered and guarded
No more room for us

When we focus only on ourselves we can only go so far. Trapped inside our own world we find limits. We can gather shiny things and heap them in piles around us to make the place more attractive but eventually we find we just have piles of shiny things. And then we have to protect them or add more just to keep up with others. Before you know it, we are no longer serving ourselves; we are serving our image or status. We can expand our world when we see the possibilities of serving a larger purpose. Then we are no longer trapped by the boundaries of our own accomplishments and sense of being.

Close your eyes and imagine a world where every being selflessly reached out to others in need in order to remove suffering. No new technology or political system or anything else is required for this to be a reality. Everything we need for this paradise already exists. It just takes inspiration and action. How ready are you to help make that a reality? What are you willing to let go of to do that? What are you willing to do to make it happen?

November 21

• • •

Guide on mountainside
Brings travelers to safety
But first he meets them

To provide compassion that matters we must first meet others at their point of need. Having our own agenda and ideas of what others need is not true compassion. While well intended that kind of help is more about propping up our own self-image. When we understand something of someone's unique suffering, and what they are capable of, we can offer the most meaningful support. Listen carefully, be curious, and tune into to what is really going on first. Then use your heart and your mind to decide what you can offer that will really matter.

November 22

• • •

Kennedy shot dead
Life can come and go quickly
Not too late to love

Nothing is certain other than we have a choice as to how we want to live. And that choice is always in front of us. Remembering that that choice might not be here tomorrow can be a sobering wake up call. And a better tomorrow is still a better tomorrow whether you are 20 or 80.

• • •

Seen but not really
Reflection on the water
Not reality

Are we seeing others as reflections of our own agenda and views or as they really are? Do we listen to what they say from our own perspective and needs, or do we listen deeply to what the reality is as experienced by them? Stepping back from our inclinations, holding our own conclusions at bay, and letting ourselves first experience the reality that others experience fosters compassion that makes a difference.

• • •

A landscape of pain
Revealed it calls more clearly
Our heart awakens

When we let the pain and suffering around us in, it calls us out. Our choices become starker. We can turn our backs on it or we can reach out. Eventually turning our back becomes harder and harder… and our compassion grows. Slow down enough to see the suffering of others and let it touch you.

November 25

• • •

Less important now
We make room for others' gain
Control surrendered

Practicing compassion requires that we serve others. To do this, we sometimes have to lower our own sense of importance in order to put greater focus on supporting someone else's well being. What we are really doing is letting go of our need to be in control. By doing so, we provide greater opportunities for their needs to be met in ways that work for them. Sometimes this means we do things differently than what our inclination was or is and we accept that.

November 26

• • •

A tiny seedling
Surrounded by giant oaks
Develops patience

Sometimes we realize how far we have to go in our efforts to be helpful. Others are more experienced, more adept, and we are just beginners. Seeing this we realize the growth we have ahead of us. When we accept this we develop the patience that allows us to be gentle with ourselves.

November 27

• • •

Sunlight, rain, and soil
Seeds sprout and wild flowers grow
Each needs the other

When people offer to make your life easier, accept
it with grace. This is an exercise in self-compassion
as you allow yourself to be supported. It is also an
exercise in compassion for others. Without your
willingness to receive their compassion they would
not have that opportunity to practice their own.

• • •

Leaves of many hues
Together the tree is made
Not the other way

It feels good to say we want to help the world. It's a noble sentiment. However, we work with details, not the finished product. Our efforts only make a difference when we make them tangible with whatever is before us. Make your compassion practice tangible with the environment that is around you. Your family, your work colleagues, your friends, your fellow commuters, your barber, the local shopkeeper... you get the picture.

• • •

Persistent question
Reminds us others are real
What is their life like?

The more we ask ourselves this question the more
compassionate we can be towards others we might
judge negatively. That really fat guy crowding out
the passengers seated next to him, the hysterical
lady creating a drama, the disheveled and spaced
out woman imposing herself on you. They all have
their own reality and are more than the story you
likely are telling yourself about them. When we
ask ourselves, in the moment, what it must be like
to be them we can sense the challenge and pain
they face and our attitude changes. Use this
question to make those around you human and to
awaken your heart to their plight.

November 30

• • •

**Soft, smooth covering
Wrapped around us we feel good
Others like it, too**

Treating ourselves well in ways that also benefits others is always a good idea. What can you do for yourself today, and every day, that meets this standard?

December

December 1

• • •

Smooth, flat water
Peaceful sea calms and inspires
Stay in harmony

Compassion can be like this. When our actions leave no wake behind us we are like the calm that flat water inspires. We are doing no harm, which is the first rule of compassion. When we move through the day like this we also provide a refuge for others who sense our calm. Be on the lookout for any waves you make around you and settle into a pace that produces harmony.

December 2

• • •

Beginning and end
Looking forward and then back
Nothing escapes us

When our first thoughts of the day embrace the open heart of compassion, and our last thoughts examine how we did, then all of our waking moments become material for developing our compassion. Make use of every moment of every day. If you acted with compassion cherish it, if you did not, learn from it so that you can do better next time.

December 3

• • •

Anchor overboard
Jerks us down as it catches
Why drop it at all?

A negative outlook is one thing. Giving voice to it
and wrapping ourselves up in the emotion is
another. Before you know it you've gotten fixated
on it and won't let go. In the meantime, any
chance of being open to others is lost. As you get
pulled down, a self-destructive cycle starts. We'll
all been there. Many times. What we do going
forward is up to us. Next time you feel that
negative outlook building, choose not to give voice
to it.

December 4

• • •

Shedding skin slowly
Unwieldy and difficult
Not new but not old

As we grow our awareness of our stance towards others and ourselves we see that we come up against old habits again and again. Despite our best intentions we may find that we instinctively focus on our self while ignoring others. It is only later that we realize we never really connected with the other person. Other times we manage to stay open to another's needs and difficulties and meet them where they really are. We find we are in between our old way of being and the new one we are developing. It's awkward and can be discouraging. It's also temporary. Recognize that you are changing and celebrate that.

December 5

• • •

Ambush comes swiftly
Laid low in a hit and run
Our heart stays open

These are challenging situations. One never knows what led to a sudden betrayal or attack from a friend or colleague. Did we miss some signs; did we bring this on our self? These can be helpful questions to learn from. However, the compassion we bring to these situations lies with our heart. Can we keep it open towards ourselves and the other person? To be sure, this doesn't mean we condone those actions or that we make ourselves a target. It does mean we hold open the possibility that we may have been to blame and accept what is ours to accept without belittling ourselves. We also hold open the possibility that the other person can develop into a better person. We do not give up on ourselves and we do not give up on others. You can start practicing this by using a past situation where you were challenged by another's unexpected behavior towards you.

December 6

• • •

Nighttime comes and goes
We rest, we recharge and rise
How else can it be?

Some days we lie low and attend to business. We
catch up, we stay close to home, and we stay out of
the fray. Without days like this how can we keep
up our pace? Without days like this how can we be
prepared to help alleviate suffering and pain in the
world? Self-compassion is the foundation of
compassion for others.

December 7

• • •

**Chasm divides the ground
We stop, ponder how to cross
Better than falling**

Imagine walking across a field and coming upon a chasm. If you kept walking you'd simply fall into the opening. If you stop and consider the situation you can come up with an answer that keeps you out of danger. The same is true in our relationships. When confronted by a challenge we can treat it like a chasm and stop and consider how we can wisely approach the other side. Doing so keeps us from falling into the chasm and creating harm to others or ourselves.

December 8

• • •

A moment in time
A leaf falls, a cloud goes by
Many lives are changed

It is the in-between moments that make up our lives. We have many short moments when we can enjoy beauty and we have many short moments when we can add beauty. The simple acts of compassion we show when we lend a helping hand, lighten a load, smile, or listen can change the direction of someone's day. In turn, that change can ripple out to others. In just the time it takes for breeze to rustle the leaves, you can touch many lives for the better. What are you waiting for?

December 9

• • •

Fighting the battle
Doing our best is enough
Another day done

When we're down on ourselves simply making it
through the day is a reminder to rejoice and
recognize that we cared enough to push on. Dwell
on that, embrace that you merited your best,
regardless of the outcome.

December 10

• • •

Ready to dive in
Vast ocean challenges us
Begin somewhere else

Our compassion can be limitless. But that doesn't
mean we should start by taking on the world.   For
one thing, the person before us is easier to relate
to than the suffering of all beings. For another,
those immediately around us will still be there and
be ready to benefit from our compassion even if
we are focused on the world. By starting local we
expand our capacity where we can get immediate
feedback and learn from our actions. The ocean
will be there for us when we are ready.

December 11

• • •

Heat seeking missile
Mission will be accomplished
Right or wrong target

What we set out to do we usually achieve. So, our intentions make a difference. Having our larger purpose in mind keeps us from choosing the wrong target. We can cut off that person trying to back out of the parking lot or we can wait ten seconds and let them out in front of us. We can listen to our son or daughter's story or we can get annoyed and cut him or her off. We can see our customer as someone in need and look for a solution or we can think about what it is costing us to serve him or her. We make these choices everyday. Does compassion serve your larger purpose? If so, stay aware of what you are trying to accomplish and let your compassion play its role. Pick some times to remind yourself of this each day.

December 12

• • •

Lightning flashes bright
Powerful, stunning, brilliant!
Sun shines all the time

Our approach to developing our compassion can be
like lightening: quick, strong, and powerful. Or, it
can be like the sun: steady, lasting, and clear.
Avoid being attached to sudden or quick growth
and take the longer view to develop a sustainable
capacity.

December 13

• • •

**Works all of the time
Downsides? None. Upsides? Boundless.
Only one way to go**

What works better than compassion at solving the world's problems? If we, all of us, always stood up for ourselves and always helped others when we could, what kind of world would we live in? Can you conceive of any scenario where the result is anything less than wonderful?

December 14

• • •

Mooring holds boat fast
True spirit checked, made captive
Pulling harder hurts

It's hard to connect with others when our sense of self, our self-ish-ness, keeps tugging at us, grabbing our attention. Fighting against it reinforces the hold it has. The struggle makes its presence all the more real. When we relax and let go we find we can move more freely. Slipping the mooring is another thing altogether. To do that we first have to practice letting go of that self-ish-ness. How do we practice this? One way is to visualize and wish for good things to go to others. We don't need to suffer ourselves but we can shift our focus towards the good of others. We can even put this into practice. Start small with letting that driver move ahead of you, or letting someone get to the end of the line before you. Make it a regular practice.

December 15

. . .

Oven bakes fresh bread
Aroma brings our heart joy
All the prize we need

The same happens when our compassion is
natural; we are filled with joy. Welcome that joy
and let it fill your heart. Let it move you towards
being an even more compassionate being.

December 16

• • •

Tick tock…tiiiick toocckkk…. tiiiiiccckk…..
Slowing down the world still turns
Still real, just more so

Stepping back from our normal pace we move with less effort and notice more. Perhaps it is the other way around. By noticing more, we seem to move more easily. When our attention is on others we become less stressed and more in tune with the world. Spend the day making the day brighter for others by noticing small opportunities as they arise. A helping hand here, a compliment there, let them happen as you spot them. See if your day isn't less stressful and if the world doesn't slow down and become more real.

共感

December 17

• • •

OK to let go
Rules that rule us do not serve
Turn them inside out

We all have disciplines that might occasionally come in conflict with living fully. When that happens we are challenged. We can keep to our good habits and drag ourselves, and probably others as well, down. Or we can temporarily break those routines and free ourselves from the conflict. Facing this choice helps us find out how much those disciplines dominate us versus serve us. If we can let those habits go without self-recrimination they are our tools and serve us. We can take them back up when the conflict has passed. If instead we find we can't let them go, or we indulge in self-recrimination when we do, we learn how much more work at self-compassion we have to do.

December 18

• • •

Same ground trod often
Worn path easy to follow
Now waits for action

With repeated practice it becomes easier to
exercise compassion. While the effort required for
this is less of a challenge, we must still practice it
for it to happen!   Letting up when we think we are
mastering anything is a sure way to diminish what
we can offer to the world and ourselves.

December 19

• • •

Sitting on the bench
Game continues anyhow
Now what do we do?

Maybe you are sick or are spending time alone or are otherwise limited in your engagement of others. It can be hard to think about compassion when we are left to ourselves. Regardless, people are still in need and we still have ourselves to support. On days like this it can be tempting to withdraw and be judgmental of us. Or we can use it as a rest or an opportunity to reflect and strengthen our intention. Or we can find another way to respond to these situations. How would you like to use these breaks in the action?

共感

December 20

• • •

Small fire breaking out
Smoldering, it threatens more
Why not ignore it?

It's hard to imagine ignoring a small fire breaking out nearby. Yet when we are not at our best, and we unload our anxiety or anger or disappointment on others, we can find it easy to overlook. While part of us knows that we behaved badly and trampled on someone else, part of us turns away and covers it up so that we don't see what we've done. Staying in touch with the uncomfortable knowledge that we just hurt someone else keeps us from ignoring it. We then know we have a choice, we can own up to what we've done and say, "I'm sorry," or we can let the situation smolder and risk it growing into an even larger problem. To say, "I'm sorry," requires us to put someone else's wellbeing ahead of protecting a false self-identity. This is the very essence of compassion, being willing to put someone ahead of yourself in order to end their pain or hurt. Practice saying I'm sorry and making amends when you know your actions were less than noble.

December 21

• • •

The sun drops quickly
Deep in the ground life sleeps
Waiting patiently

Compassion is a long-term project. The winter
months provide a safe haven for life, holding it
until the time is right. So too can we nurture our
own life, protecting it when conditions are harsh,
knowing a better time awaits. What must change
for our own life spirit to grow? What can we set
into motion today, and work with in the coming
months, to create a better environment for our
own unfolding? Write it down someplace where
you will be regularly reminded of it and motivated
by it.

共感

December 22

• • •

Boogeyman ahead
We disdain him and his ilk
Then we see deeper

When we pay attention we may find we automatically think poorly of certain people. Maybe we think fat people are lazy, maybe we think skinny people are inbred, maybe we think Republicans are Luddites, maybe we think Democrats are deluded, maybe we think others are stupid or shallow or nerds, or whatever because of how they dress or look. Right away we have an opinion; and then we look with an open heart and mind. What might explain why they are the way they are? If they truly are hateful, or hurtful, or suffering we ask ourselves how we might help them. Can we wish them well? Here is where our compassion is tested and grown. These opportunities to grow our compassion come to us everyday. We can be thankful for them and use them.

• • •

Soft steps lightly tread
Little trace of wear and tear
We all benefit

How we approach others impacts their day. When
we show up prepared, patient, and thoughtful,
others benefit. And so do we.

December 24

• • •

Sprout pushing through soil
Progress unseen and trying
No other way up

Sometimes working to expand our compassion is just downright hard. We aren't as aware as we'd like, it may feel like we are taking one step forward and two steps back, and the results are hard to see. Think of the seedling pushing through the soil in its march towards the sun.   The steady effort is unseen and arduous but a necessary step that is simply a part of the process. Keep your efforts steady regardless of the challenges of the day.

December 25

• • •

No self-awareness
All being done for others
No more obstacles

Compassion flows spontaneously when we are so
absorbed in boosting the welfare of others that we
lose any sense or attachment to a self. Keep your
sole focus on how the lives of others can change
for the better.

December 26

• • •

Tar pits all around
Stepping in muck we get stuck
Leave our shoes behind

When someone unexpectedly treats us in a way we find offensive we can get stuck trying to figure out what was going on. As sincere as we are in trying to not become judgmental or defensive or annoyed we are still trying. And the more we try, the more we get stuck. Maybe it's a little pride or sense of over-inflated sense of self that keeps us stuck. Leave it behind like you would your shoes if you were stuck in tar. Freed once more we can connect with what is more important.

December 27

• • •

Rich colors warm us
Life is more vivid and real
Waiting to be seen

The goodness in others and in us is always there.
When we look for it we find it. And when we do
life becomes richer and more engaging. When that
happens we more naturally reach out to support
others and are kinder to ourselves. Stop for a
moment to look for the good.

• • •

Purring cat on lap
Warmth magically appears
Goodness discovered

When a purring cat curls on our lap the impact is obvious. Whatever mood existed before is now made better. There is a lesson there. How we treat others has an impact on the goodness we can find in them. Waiting for that goodness to appear on its own can sometimes take a very long time. We can find it quicker by how we see and treat those around us. Connecting with that goodness sets the conditions for compassion to be flourish.

December 29

• • •

Darkness all around
We do not see the flowers
Then our eyes open

Everyday, all around us are opportunities to learn about love for others and ourselves. Whether or not we see them is up to us. We can get so used to operating on habit and conditioned responses that we fail to see what is right before us. Part of growing compassion is learning from our experiences. How are we treating others and why? What do we do when we have the opportunity to support those we love, much less those we don't know? Why do we hate or disdain others, what do we really know about them. Until we explore these questions we continue to walk around life as if our eyes are closed.

December 30

• • •

Child strikes out at us
Evokes not anger, but love
Why not for adults?

There are times when others bitterly oppose us.
They attack what we think, say, and do. If they
were a child we would know that their anger is
borne not of ill will but of their circumstances. The
same can be true for adults. Seeing that there
might be terrible experiences that explain their
behavior helps move us from anger and desire for
revenge to wanting to understand them better and
wanting to help them. Step back and take the
larger view. If nothing else, be glad that you are
not them. You're likely to find your heart softens
and allows you to take an entirely more
compassionate stance.

December 31

• • •

Sun is shining bright
Natural and essential
Its light reaches all

This is my wish for you. May your compassion grow and be like the sun. Let it shine brightly to reach all. That we need it is undeniable. It is essential for the growth and wellbeing of all. Indeed, it is the only thing that can end the suffering of the world.

5165141R10212

Made in the USA
San Bernardino, CA
31 October 2013